lifetogether
publishing

# DEEPENING
# LIFE
# TOGETHER

# ROMANS

## LIFE TOGETHER

**BakerBooks**
*a division of Baker Publishing Group*
Grand Rapids, Michigan

*Lamplighter Media*

Published by Lamplighter Media
6755 Mira Mesa Blvd. #123-272
San Diego, CA 92121
www.GroupSpice.com

Printed in the United States of America

Library of Congress Cataloging-in-Publication Data
Romans / [editors, Mark L. Strauss, Teresa Haymaker].
    p.  cm. — (Deepening life together)
    Includes bibliographical references.
    ISBN 978-1-941326-25-1 (pbk.)
    1. Bible. N.T. Romans—Textbooks. 2. Bible. N.T. Romans—Study and teaching.
    I. Strauss, Mark L. II. Haymaker, Teresa.
    BS2665.55.R66 2009
    227'.10071—dc22                        2009014856

# CONTENTS

3

# ACKNOWLEDGMENTS

The *Deepening Life Together: Romans* Small Group Video Bible Study has come together through the efforts of many at Baker Publishing Group, Lifetogether Publishing, and Lamplighter Media, for which we express our heartfelt thanks.

| | |
|---|---|
| Executive Producer | John Nill |
| Producer and Director | Sue Doc Ross |
| Editors | Mark L. Strauss (Scholar), Teresa Haymaker |
| Curriculum Development | Rob DeKlotz, Brett Eastman, Pam Marotta, Stephanie French, Teresa Haymaker, Karen Lee-Thorp |
| Video Production | Chris Balish, Rodney Bissell, Nick Calabrese, Sebastian Hoppe Fuentes, Josh Greene, Patrick Griffin, Teresa Haymaker, Oziel Jabin Ibarra, Natali Ibarra, Janae Janik, Keith Sorrell, Lance Tracy |
| Teachers and Scholars | Lynn Cohick, Andrew Hill, Moyer Hubbard, Joanne Jung, Jon Laansma, Nick Perrin, Greg Sidders, Mark Strauss, Erik Thoennes |
| Baker Publishing Group | Jack Kuhatschek |

Special thanks to DeLisa Ivy, Bethel Seminary, Talbot School of Theology, Wheaton College

Interior icons by Tom Clark

Most people want to live a healthy, balanced spiritual life, but few achieve this by themselves. And most small groups struggle to balance all of God's purposes in their meetings. Groups tend to overemphasize one of the five purposes, perhaps fellowship or discipleship. Rarely is there a healthy balance that includes evangelism, ministry, and worship. That's why we've included all of these elements in this study so you can live a healthy, balanced spiritual life over time.

A typical group session will include the following:

## Memory Verses

For each session we have provided a memory verse that emphasizes an important truth from the session. This is an optional exercise, but we believe that memorizing Scripture can be a vital part of filling our minds with God's Word. We encourage you to give this important habit a try.

## CONNECTING *with God's Family (Fellowship)*

The foundation for spiritual growth is an intimate connection with God and his family. A few people who really know you and who earn your trust provide a place to experience the life Jesus invites you to live. This section of each session typically offers you two activities. You can get to know your whole group by using the icebreaker question, and/or you can check in with one or two group members—your spiritual partner(s)—for a deeper connection and encouragement in your spiritual journey.

DVD TEACHING SEGMENT. A *Deepening Life Together: Romans* Video Teaching DVD companion to this study guide is available. For each study session, the DVD contains a lesson taught by Greg Sidders. If you are using the DVD, you will view the teaching segment after your *Connecting* discussion and before your group discussion time (the *Growing* section). At the end of each session in this study guide you will find space for your notes on the teaching segment.

## GROWING *to Be Like Christ (Discipleship)*

Here is where you come face-to-face with Scripture. In core passages you'll explore what the Bible teaches about the topic of the study. The focus won't be on accumulating information but on how we should live in light of the Word of God. We want to help you apply the Scriptures practically, creatively, and from your heart as well as your head. At the end of the day, allowing the timeless truths from God's Word to transform our lives in Christ is our greatest aim.

## DEVELOPING *Your Gifts to Serve Others (Ministry)*

Jesus trained his disciples to discover and develop their gifts to serve others. And God has designed each of us uniquely to serve him in a way no other person can. This section will help you discover and use your God-given design. It will also encourage your group to discover your unique design as a community. In this study, you'll put into practice what you've learned in the Bible study by taking a step to serve others. These simple steps will take your group on a faith journey that could change your lives forever.

## SHARING *Your Life Mission Every Day (Evangelism)*

Many people skip over this aspect of the Christian life because it's scary, relationally awkward, or simply too much work for their busy schedules. But Jesus wanted all of his disciples to help outsiders connect with him, to know him personally. This doesn't mean preaching on street corners. It could mean welcoming a few newcomers into your group, hosting a short-term group in your home, or walking through this study with a friend. In this study, you'll have an opportunity to go beyond Bible study to biblical living.

## SURRENDERING *Your Life for God's Pleasure (Worship)*

God is most pleased by a heart that is fully his. Each group session will give you a chance to surrender your heart to God in prayer and worship. You may read a psalm together, share a page in your journal, or sing a song to close your meeting. If you have never prayed aloud in a group before, no one will pressure you. Instead, you'll experience the support of others who are praying for you.

## Study Notes

This section provides background notes on the Bible passage(s) you examine in the *Growing* section. You may want to refer to these notes during your group meeting or as a reference for those doing additional study.

## For Deeper Study (Optional)

If you want to dig deeper into more Bible passages about the topic at hand, we've provided additional passages and questions. Your group may choose to do study homework ahead of each meeting in order to cover more biblical material. Or you as an individual may choose to study the *For Deeper Study* on your own. If you prefer not to do study homework, the *Growing* section will provide you with plenty to discuss within the group. These options allow individuals or the whole group to go deeper in their study, while still accommodating those who can't do homework or are new to your group.

You can record your discoveries in your journal. We encourage you to read some of your insights to a friend (spiritual partner) for accountability and support. Spiritual partners may check in each week over the phone, through e-mail, or at the beginning of the group meeting.

## Reflections

On the *Reflections* pages we provide Scriptures to read and reflect on between group meetings. We suggest you use this section to seek God at home throughout the week. This time at home should begin and end with prayer. Don't get in a hurry; take enough time to hear God's direction.

## Subgroup for Discussion and Prayer

If your group is large (more than seven people), we encourage you to separate into groups of two to four for discussion and prayer. This is to encourage greater participation and deeper discussion.

# INTRODUCTION

Welcome to the *Deepening Life Together* Bible study on the book of *Romans*. We will experience life together these next seven weeks as the apostle Paul leads us through his greatest theological work—his magnum opus—written to the church in Rome. The journey we are about to embark on will take us step-by-step through the truth of the gospel as it relates to the topics of condemnation, justification, and sanctification. As we read, discuss, and reflect on the topic of each session, we will be encouraged to give ourselves completely to God and live lives in appropriate response to God's greatest gift of salvation and worthy of our new position in Jesus Christ.

Week by week, we will see Paul's doctrine of justification revealed through the pages of Scripture as we learn first what it means to be condemned and how we came to be in that condition. Secondly, we will discover how we, as human beings unable to save ourselves, can be brought back into a relationship with God by being declared righteous through faith in Jesus Christ's sacrificial death on the cross. Finally, in the climax and resolution to the study, we will discover how, having been freed from our bondage to sin, the Law, and death, to live our new lives through the power of the Spirit.

This journey of discovery will make known God's purposes for our lives. We will connect with our loving and faithful God and with other believers in small group community. We will become his hands and feet here on earth as he reveals our uniqueness and his willingness to use us. We will experience the closeness that he desires with

11

us as we prayerfully respond to the principles we learn in this study and learn to place him first in our lives.

We at Baker Books and Lifetogether Publishing look forward to hearing the stories of how God changes you from the inside out during this small group experience. We pray God blesses you with all he has planned for you through this journey together.

> For the LORD is good and his love endures forever;
> his faithfulness continues through all generations.

> Psalm 100:5 (NIV)

# AN INTRODUCTION TO ROMANS

**Memory Verse: But now a righteousness from God, apart from law, has been made known, to which the Law and the Prophets testify. This righteousness from God comes through faith in Jesus Christ to all who believe (Rom. 3:21–22 NIV).**

On October 31, 1517, Martin Luther nailed his renowned Ninety-Five Theses to the door of the All Saint's Church in Wittenberg, Germany. Convinced that the church of his day had become corrupted, Luther, a German monk and theologian, contested the teaching of his contemporaries through his theses.

Centuries earlier, the apostle Paul had explained how we are justified. Justification (or righteousness) is an image from the law courts. It means being acquitted of crimes. It also means being restored to right relationship with the person we have wronged—in this case, God. Normally a judge acquits someone because that person is innocent, but as we will see in Romans, God has made a way to satisfy the demands of justice while still acquitting us, even though we are guilty.

## Connecting

As you begin *Session One*, ask the Lord in prayer to unify your group and challenge you as you study his Word during these next seven weeks.

Take time to pass around a copy of the *Small Group Roster*, a sheet of paper, or one of you pass your study guide, opened to the *Small Group Roster*. Each of you write down your contact information including the best time and method for contacting you. Then, someone volunteer to make copies or type up a list with everyone's information and e-mail it to the group this week.

1. Begin this first session by introducing yourselves. Include your name, what you do for a living, and what you do for fun. You may also include whether or not you are married, how long you have been married, how many children you have, and their ages. Also share what brought you to this small group study of Romans, and what you expect to learn during the next seven weeks.

2. Whether your group is new or ongoing, it's always important to reflect on and review your values together. In the *Appendix* is a *Small Group Agreement* with the values most useful in sustaining healthy, balanced groups. Choose two or three values that you have room to grow in or haven't previously focused on—to emphasize during this study. Doing this will take your group to the next stage of intimacy and spiritual health.

3. When you were a child and you did something wrong, how did you and your parents generally deal with the situation?

## Growing

Central to the development of a first-century theology and ethic, Paul's letter to the church in Rome is considered by many to be his greatest theological work and the greatest of all the epistles. It is loved for its wonderful exposition of Christian doctrines as well as its practical exhortations to Christian life.

4. Romans is Paul's statement of the gospel, the good news that God has sent Paul to proclaim to the world. What can we learn about this news from 1:1–5, 16–17? What questions do these statements about the gospel raise for you?

5. Faith is an important word in Romans. See the Study Note on faith. What does obedience have to do with faith (1:5)?

6. Another central term in Romans is righteousness (1:17). God is perfectly just, so people who behave unjustly can't have a close relationship with him. Do you think God (and his followers) should just get over making such a big deal about righteousness or justice, and talk about love instead? Explain your thoughts.

7. Jesus and his first followers were all Jews. Paul was Jewish too. But part of Paul's calling was to invite non-Jews (Gentiles) to the intimate relationship with God that until then had been for Jews only. This was a radical idea at the time, and Paul spends a lot of time in Romans explaining how Jews and Gentiles each fit into the amazing good news he proclaims. What does he say about each group in 1:16; 2:9–11?

8. Are you a Jew or a Gentile? Does it matter to you that Jesus was Jewish, that the Scriptures were first given to Jews, and that God enabled Gentiles to get in on the gift of this Jewish Savior? How, or why not?

9. One of Paul's purposes in writing Romans was to make the case that everyone, Jew and Gentile alike, is guilty before God because of their sin. Look at the following fourteen key arguments Paul makes in Romans 3:10–18 regarding sin.

> There is no one righteous, not even one;
> there is no one who understands, no one who seeks God.

All have turned away, they have together become worthless;
there is no one who does good, not even one.
Their throats are open graves; their tongues practice deceit.
The poison of vipers is on their lips.
Their mouths are full of cursing and bitterness.
Their feet are swift to shed blood; ruin and misery mark their
     ways,
and the way of peace they do not know.
There is no fear of God before their eyes. (NIV)

Why is it so important to understand that everyone is sinful and guilty before God, regardless of their background or beliefs? (See Romans 3:19–20 for help.)

10. The law given to the Jews in the Old Testament demonstrated that all people, Jews and Gentiles, were lawbreakers at their core. Now read Romans 3:21–22. What do we learn from these verses about how both Jews and Gentiles become right with God? See the Study Notes for more information about salvation and faith.

11. We are made right with God by faith in Jesus Christ. In Romans 6–8, Paul shows how we then live by faith in Jesus Christ through the empowering presence of the Holy Spirit. Read Romans 8:26–30. What does Paul say here about our new life in the Holy Spirit?

12. In Romans 12–15, Paul describes what life by faith in Christ, in the power of the Holy Spirit, looks like. How does he summarize the life of faith in 12:1–2?

13. This has been a fast overview of some of the highlights of this book! What is one insight you come away with, one question you need to pursue, or one thing you need to do or think about differently?

Paul wrote Romans to the church in Rome while in Corinth on his third missionary journey. He wanted to share the gospel message with the Romans and solicit their support for his outreach into Spain.

The theme of Romans, the gospel message, is reflected throughout the book. In the next six sessions of this study we will explore Paul's systematic presentation of the gospel that he had been preaching for more than twenty years, as well as the practical application of the gospel in everyday life.

## Developing

God has given every believer special gifts to be used for serving him and the body of Christ as the Holy Spirit leads. As we strive to deepen our relationship with him through prayer, reflection, and meditation on his Word, we begin developing the gifts that God has given each of us. Through these disciplines, we learn how to hear his still small voice and submit to the leading of the Holy Spirit.

14. Developing our ability to serve God according to the leading of the Holy Spirit requires that we make time to let God speak to us daily. Which of the following next steps toward this goal are you willing to take for the next few weeks?

    ☐ *Prayer.* Commit to connecting with God daily through personal prayer. It's important to separate yourself from the distractions in your life so you can really focus on communicating with God. Some people find it helpful to write out their prayers in a journal.

    ☐ *Reflection.* At the end of each session you'll find *Reflections* Scriptures that specifically relate to the topic of our study each week. These are provided to give you an opportunity for reading a short Bible passage five days a week during the course of this study. Write down your insights on what you read each day in the space provided. On the sixth day, summarize what God has shown you throughout the week.

    ☐ *Meditation.* Meditation is focused attention on the Word of God and is a great way to internalize God's Word more deeply. Copy a portion of Scripture on a card and tape it somewhere in your line of sight, such as your car's dashboard or the kitchen table. Think about it when you sit at red lights, or while you're eating a meal. Reflect on what God is saying to you through these words. Several passages for meditation are suggested on the *Reflections* pages in each session.

## Surrendering

Worship means to revere or adore God. Hebrews 12:28–29 says, "Therefore, since we are receiving a kingdom that cannot be shaken, let us be thankful, and so worship God acceptably with reverence and awe, for our 'God is a consuming fire'" (NIV). As receivers of his kingdom, let's offer praise to our God, as he deserves.

15. Spend a few minutes praising God aloud. You may highlight some of the attributes of God's character or praise him for specific circumstances in your life.

   ☐ Someone offer your musical gifts to lead the group in a worship song. You might try singing a simple chorus a cappella, with guitar or piano accompaniment, or with a worship CD.

   ☐ Read a passage of Scripture aloud together, making it a time of praise and worship as the words remind you of all God has done for you. Choose a psalm or other favorite verse.

16. Every believer should have a plan for spending time alone with God. Your time with God is individual and reflects who you are in relationship with our personal God. However you choose to spend your time with him, try to allow time for praise, prayer, and reading of Scripture.

   At the end of each session we provide *Reflections* for you to use in your daily time with him. There are five daily Scripture readings with space to record your thoughts. On the sixth day there is space to record your summary of the five reflections. These will offer reinforcement of the principles we are learning, and develop or strengthen your habit of time alone with God throughout the week.

17. Before you close your group in prayer, answer this question: "How can we pray for you this week?" Write prayer requests on your *Prayer and Praise Report* and commit to praying for each other throughout the week.

## Study Notes

*Faith:* A belief in or confident attitude toward God, involving commitment to his will for one's life. Genuine saving faith is a personal attachment to Christ, best thought of as a combination of two ideas—reliance on Christ and commitment to him. Saving faith involves personally depending on the finished work of Christ's sacrifice as the only basis for forgiveness of sin and a right relationship with God.

*Salvation:* Deliverance from the power of sin; redemption. The salvation that comes through Christ may be described in three tenses: past, present, and future. When we believe in Christ, we are saved (Acts 16:31). But we are also in the process of being saved from the power of sin (Rom. 8:13; Phil. 2:12). Finally, we shall be saved from the very presence of sin (Rom. 13:11; Titus 2:12–13).

## For Deeper Study (Optional)

1. Before he became a Christian, Paul went by his Jewish name, Saul. Read Acts 7:54–8:2, in which for the first time a Jewish Christian was killed in Jerusalem for saying that Jesus was the Messiah. What do you learn about Saul/Paul?
2. Read Acts 9:1–19. What moved Saul/Paul to change? What might this experience have been like for him?
3. Read Acts 9:20–30. What was Paul like as a brand-new Christian?

4. Read Galatians 1:13–16; 2:15–20. How does Paul describe the transformation when a Jew stops relying on the Law of Moses for acceptance from God? What might it have been like for Paul, a devout Jew, to come to grips with the possibility that Christ had changed the rules, welcomed Gentiles, and made law-keeping irrelevant? What does his story say to you about your life? What light does his story shed on what he says in Romans about Jews and Gentiles? About law and grace?

## Reflections

Reading, reflecting, and meditating on the Word of God is essential to getting to know him deeply. As you read the verses each day, give prayerful consideration to what you learn about God, his Spirit, and his place in your life. Then record your thoughts, insights, or prayer in the *Reflect* section below the verses you read. On the sixth day, record a summary of what you learned over the entire week through this study.

*Day 1.* I am not ashamed of the gospel, because it is the power of God for the salvation of everyone who believes: first for the Jew, then for the Gentile. For in the gospel a righteousness from God is revealed, a righteousness that is by faith from first to last, just as it is written: "The righteous will live by faith" (Rom. 1:16–17 NIV).

REFLECT

_____

_____

_____

_____

*Day 2.* Consequently, just as the result of one trespass was condemnation for all men, so also the result of one act of righteousness was justification that brings life for all men (Rom. 5:18 NIV).

REFLECT

_____

_____

_____

_____

*Day 3.* For what the law was powerless to do in that it was weakened by the sinful nature, God did by sending his own Son in the likeness of sinful man to be a sin offering. And so he condemned sin in sinful man, in order that the righteous requirements of the law might be fully met in us, who do not live according to the sinful nature but according to the Spirit (Rom. 8:3–4 NIV).

REFLECT

_____

_____

_____

_____

*Day 4.* Therefore, I urge you, brothers, in view of God's mercy, to offer your bodies as living sacrifices, holy and pleasing to God—this is your spiritual act of worship. Do not conform any longer to the pattern of this world, but be transformed by the renewing of your mind. Then you will be able to test and approve what God's will is—his good, pleasing and perfect will (Rom. 12:1–2 NIV).

REFLECT

_____

_____

_____

_____

**Day 5.** Now to him who is able to establish you by my gospel and the proclamation of Jesus Christ, according to the revelation of the mystery hidden for long ages past, but now revealed and made known through the prophetic writings by the command of the eternal God, so that all nations might believe and obey him—to the only wise God be glory forever through Jesus Christ! Amen (Rom. 16:25–27 NIV).

REFLECT

_____

_____

_____

_____

**Day 6.** Use the following space to write any insight God has put in your heart and mind about the things we have looked at in this session and during your _Reflections_ time this week.

SUMMARY

_____

_____

_____

_____

# CONDEMNATION
## HUMANITY'S NEED OF RIGHTEOUSNESS

**Memory Verse: You, therefore, have no excuse, you who pass judgment on someone else, for at whatever point you judge the other, you are condemning yourself, because you who pass judgment do the same things [Rom. 2:1 NIV].**

One of Britain's most famous judges was Sir Norman Birkett, who eventually became one of the judges at the Nuremberg trials. Birkett was known throughout London for his acerbic wit. One day a minor criminal was brought before the bench to make his final statement before sentencing.

"As God is my judge," said the man, "I'm innocent!"

Birkett replied, "He isn't, I am, and you aren't!"*

God wasn't the man's judge on that day, but one day he will be. In Romans 1:18–3:20, Paul describes the final judgment, the future day in which every person will stand before the divine court. In these chapters, we discover the principles by which God will judge the world.

It may seem strange to begin a book on God's grace by discussing his judgment. But in fact, Paul will spend these first three chapters of Romans explaining the reasons for God's wrath and judgment before he returns to talking about the Gospel. Why? Because Paul knows that we will never appreciate what it means to be saved until we know how lost we were. We will never appreciate the life Jesus offers us until we grasp the death we all deserve. And we will never

---

* Walter Cronkite, *A Reporter's Life* (New York: Knopf, 1996), 127.

appreciate the good news of the Gospel until we are confronted with the bad news about ourselves.

## Connecting

Begin your group time with prayer, inviting the Holy Spirit to join you and take charge of this meeting.

1. If you have new people joining you for the first time, take a few minutes to briefly introduce yourselves.

2. Most people want to live a healthy, balanced life. A regular medical check-up is a good way to measure health and spot potential problems. In the same way, a spiritual check-up is vital to your spiritual well-being. The *Personal Health Assessment* was designed to give you a quick snapshot, or pulse, of your spiritual health. Take a few minutes individually to complete the *Personal Health Assessment* in the *Appendix*. After answering each question, tally your results. Then, pair up with another person and briefly share one purpose area where you are strong and one that needs a little work.

3. Healthy small groups *rotate leadership*. We recommend that you rotate leaders on a regular basis. This practice helps to develop every member's ability to shepherd a few people within a safe environment. Even Jesus gave others the opportunity to serve alongside him (Mark 6:30–44).

   It's also a good idea to *rotate host homes*, with the host of each meeting providing the refreshments. Some groups like to let the host lead the meeting each week, while others like to allow one person to host while another person leads.

   The *Small Group Calendar* is a tool for planning who will lead and host each meeting. Take a few minutes to plan leaders and hosts for your remaining meetings. Don't pass this opportunity up! It will revolutionize your group. For information on leading your group, see the *Leader's Notes* introduction in the *Appendix*. Also, if you are leading for the first time, see *Leading*

24

*for the First Time (Leadership 101)* in the *Appendix*. If you still have questions about rotating hosts and/or homes, refer to the *Frequently Asked Questions (FAQs)* in the *Appendix*.

4. How might watching the evening news for a week influence your opinion about the goodness or atrocities of humanity in general?

## Growing

In these chapters, Paul shows that 1) God has a very reasonable standard of the way humans ought to live; 2) both Jews and Gentiles, in their different ways, live way below that standard; 3) therefore, both deserve judgment. Neither human effort nor membership in the covenant people of Israel can earn salvation from God's well-deserved anger.

Please read Romans 1:18–20 aloud.

5. In what ways does creation speak to people everywhere about God's existence and power?

6. Notice the phrases "although they knew," "they exchanged," and "God gave them over" in the chart below. Based on these phrases, how would you summarize humanity's sin?

| "Although they knew . . ." | ". . . they exchanged" | "God gave them over . . ." |
|---|---|---|
| Although they knew God . . . (v. 21) Although they claimed to be wise . . . (v. 22) Although they know God's righteous de-cree . . . (v. 32) | They . . . exchanged the glory of the immortal God . . . (v. 23) They exchanged the truth of God for a lie . . . (v. 25) They exchanged natural relations for unnatural ones . . . (v. 26) | God gave them over . . . to sexual impurity . . . (v. 24) God gave them over to shameful lusts . . . (v. 26) He gave them over to a depraved mind . . . (v. 28) |

What do theses phrases above tell you about the depth of people's self-deceit?

In Romans 1, Paul was describing the lifestyle of pagans in the Roman Empire. His Jewish readers might well think, "Sure, that's how the pagans live. But we Jews don't practice idolatry or sexual depravity. We follow the Law of Moses, which God gave us, so we're fine with God." Many "good" people today might well say something similar. So now Paul talks to them. Read Romans chapter 2.

7. What faults does Paul find with his fellow Jews—and by extension, with other "good" people—in Romans 2? See the Study Notes for more information about the Law of Moses.

In what ways do we in the church today judge others? How do you think God views our judgmental hearts?

Paul singles out *self-seeking* (2:8 NIV) as a serious sin. What's wrong with being self-seeking?

Non-Christians eagerly point to cases of adultery, divorce, financial cheating, racism, materialism, and other sins of professing Christians to show that Christians don't practice what they preach. How do you think we should respond when *God's name is blasphemed among the Gentiles because of* the behavior of professing Christians (2:24 NIV)?

8. God is a God of truth, and an impartial judge. What does Romans 2:6–16 say about his justice and what his criteria will be on the Day of Judgment? See the *Study Notes* for information about judgment and wrath.

Now, read Romans 3:1–20.

9. Having shown that Jews are no better than Gentiles when it comes to pleasing God, Paul knows that his readers will be asking whether there is any value at all in being a Jew. According to 3:1–2, what advantage do the Jews have that the pagans don't? Why is this such a huge head start in a relationship with God? Why do you suppose this didn't make the Jews successful in pleasing God?

10. In Romans 3:9–20, Paul quotes a number of Old Testament passages that speak of humanity's nature. How fair a description of people today do you think this is? Explain.

11. Reflect on your life and tendencies apart from Christ. Were or are you like the pagans? Like the Jews? Different from both? In what ways?

## Developing

This small group is a wonderful place for us to confront inconsistencies between what we say we believe and the way we live. As a group, commit to holding each other accountable in areas you desire growth.

12. We strongly recommend each of you partner with someone in the group to help you in your spiritual journey during this study. This person will be your "spiritual partner" for the next several weeks. Pair up with someone in your group now (men partner with men and women with women) and turn to the *Personal Health Plan.*

    In the box that says, "WHO are you connecting with spiritually?" write your partner's name. In the box that says, "WHAT is your next step for growth?" write one step you would like to take for growth during this study. Tell your partner what step you chose. When you check in with your partner each week, the "Partner's Progress" column on this chart will provide a place to record your partner's progress in the goal he or she chose.

13. Spending time getting to know each other outside of group meetings is helpful to building stronger relationships within your group. Discuss whether your group would like to have a potluck or other type of social to celebrate together what God is doing in your group. You could plan to share a meal prior to a small group meeting or plan to follow your completion of this study with a barbecue. Appoint one or two people who can follow up with everyone outside of group time to put a plan together.

## Sharing

Jesus lived and died so that mankind might come to know him intimately. His final words before his ascension as recorded in Acts 1:8 were, "You will receive power when the Holy Spirit comes on you; and you will be my witnesses in Jerusalem, and in all Judea and Samaria, and to the ends of the earth" (NIV). Through the Holy Spirit, we are empowered to be his witnesses to those around us.

14. Today's study has been all about the idea that no one is righteous enough to earn God's favor. How would you explain this idea to a person who believes that he or she is good and not guilty of any serious sins? (See Rom. 3:9–20 for help.)

15. Use the *Circles of Life* diagram below to help you think of people you come in contact with on a regular basis who need

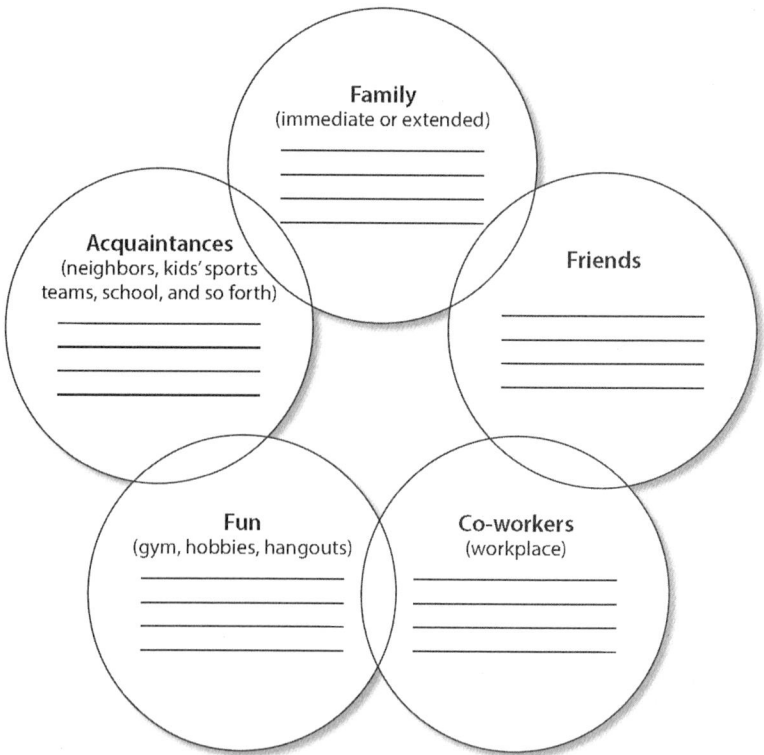

**Family**
(immediate or extended)

**Acquaintances**
(neighbors, kids' sports teams, school, and so forth)

**Friends**

**Fun**
(gym, hobbies, hangouts)

**Co-workers**
(workplace)

to be connected in Christian community. Write at least two names in each circle.

The people who fill these circles are not there by accident. God has strategically placed each of them within your sphere of influence because he has equipped you to minister to them and share with them in ways no one else can. Consider the following ideas for reaching out to one or two of the people you listed and make a plan to follow through with them this week.

☐ This is a wonderful time to welcome a few friends into your group. Which of the people you listed could you invite? It's possible that you may need to help your friend overcome obstacles to coming to a place where he or she can encounter Jesus. Does your friend need a ride to the group or help with childcare?

☐ Consider inviting a friend to attend a weekend church service with you and possibly plan to enjoy a meal together afterward. This can be a great opportunity to talk with someone about your faith in Jesus.

☐ Is there someone who is unable to attend your group but who still needs a connection? Would you be willing to have lunch or coffee with that person, catch up on life, and share something you've learned from this study? Jesus doesn't call all of us to lead small groups, but he does call every disciple to spiritually multiply his or her life over time.

## Surrendering

This may have been a difficult session for some, but the very nature of God demands justice. The good news is that he did not leave us in a state of condemnation. In the next session we will see God's provision for making us righteous. We can be thankful and praise the Lord for his faithfulness to us in spite of our sinful nature.

16. Read Romans 2:29: "For God is not looking for those who cut their bodies in actual body circumcision, but he is looking for

those with changed hearts and minds. Whoever has that kind of change in his life will get his praise from God, even if not from you" (TLB). Thank God in prayer for this or another verse that encouraged you in this session. Consider how you can thank God daily over the next week.

17. Take a few minutes to talk about what it would take to make time with God a priority every day or even five or six days a week. Don't have expectations for time at first; consider drawing near to God for a few minutes each day and gradually you will desire more. Use the *Reflections* at the end of each session for drawing near to God.

18. Share your prayer requests in your group and then gather in smaller circles of three or four people to pray. Be sure to write down the personal requests of each member to use as a reminder to pray for your group throughout the week.

    Then pray for one another in your circle. Don't put pressure on anyone to pray aloud. As you pray, you may find it meaningful to hold hands or place your hands on another person's shoulder. Jesus often touched people to communicate his care for them.

## Study Notes

*Law of Moses (Mosaic Law):* In the Old Testament, a unique law code was established by direct revelation from God to direct his people in their worship, in their relationship to him, and in their social relationships with one another.

The Mosaic Law came from God through Moses, issued from his nature, and was holy, righteous, and good. These laws were binding on his people. God depicts his law as an expression of his love for his people (Exod. 19:5–6).

Biblical law is more than a record of human law. It is an expression of what God requires of human beings. It rests on the eternal moral principles that are consistent with the very nature of God himself. Therefore, biblical law is the summary of moral law. As such it sets forth fundamental and universal moral principles.

*Righteousness:* The Greek word translated "righteousness" in Romans 1:17 and 3:5 can carry the sense of moral righteousness or societal justice. For Paul, righteousness is conformity with God's perfect standards. Since humans are too selfish and flawed to stick to such standards by sheer will-power, righteousness must be received as a gift from God on the basis of Christ's sacrificial death on the cross.

*Judgment:* Judgment in this context refers to a judicial pronouncement or sentence resulting in punishment. Paul warns that those who pronounce others guilty will themselves be judged guilty.

*Wrath:* By "wrath" Paul means a state of indignation directed at wrongdoing. God's righteous wrath results in punishment to the wrongdoer.

## For Deeper Study [Optional]

To understand clearly some of the things that kindle God's wrath and evoke his judgment, go back and read Romans 1:18–2:12. Look for the kinds of things that are referred to as ungodly or unrighteous, and things that will meet with God's judgment.

1. Which of those things do people today consider acceptable?

2. In light of what you know about the character of God, how do you think God wants us to live in the midst of a culture that often fails to respect his standards of righteousness?

# Reflections

Hopefully last week you made a commitment to read, reflect and meditate on the Word of God each day. Following are selections of Scripture provided as a starting point to drawing near to God through time with him. Read the daily verses and then record your thoughts, insights, or prayers in the space provided. On the sixth day, record a summary of what you have learned over the entire week through this study or use this space to write down how God has challenged you personally.

*Day 1.* You, therefore, have no excuse, you who pass judgment on someone else, for at whatever point you judge the other, you are condemning yourself, because you who pass judgment do the same things (Rom. 2:1 NIV).

REFLECT

_____

_____

_____

_____

*Day 2.* No, a true Jew is one whose heart is right with God. And true circumcision is not merely obeying the letter of the law; rather, it is a change of heart produced by God's Spirit. And a person with a changed heart seeks praise from God, not from people (Rom. 2:29 NLT).

REFLECT

_____

_____

_____

_____

*Day 3.* Don't you see how wonderfully kind, tolerant, and patient God is with you? Does this mean nothing to you? Can't you see that his kindness is intended to turn you from your sin? (Rom. 2:4 NLT).

REFLECT

_____

_____

_____

_____

**Day 4.** He will give eternal life to those who keep on doing good, seeking after the glory and honor and immortality that God offers (Rom. 2:7 NLT).

REFLECT

_____

_____

_____

_____

**Day 5.** Obviously, the law applies to those to whom it was given, for its purpose is to keep people from having excuses, and to show that the entire world is guilty before God. For no one can ever be made right with God by doing what the law commands. The law simply shows us how sinful we are (Rom. 3:19–20 NLT).

REFLECT

_____

_____

_____

_____

***Day* 6.** Use this space to record insights, thoughts, or prayers that God has given you during *Session Two* and your *Reflections* time.

SUMMARY

_____

_____

_____

_____

# JUSTIFICATION
## SALVATION THROUGH FAITH ALONE

**Memory Verse: This righteousness from God comes through faith in Jesus Christ to all who believe (Rom. 3:22 NIV).**

Jonah was a prophet chosen by God to deliver a message of certain destruction to the city of Nineveh. Rather than obey God, Jonah ran in the opposite direction, to Tarshish. Jonah 4:2 gives us the reason: "He prayed to the LORD, 'O LORD, is this not what I said when I was still at home? That is why I was so quick to flee to Tarshish. I knew that you are a gracious and compassionate God, slow to anger and abounding in love, a God who relents from sending calamity'" (NIV). The truth is, Jonah wanted the evil people to get what they deserved, not grace from a compassionate God.

Ultimately, Jonah obeyed the Lord and preached the message to the Ninevites, who received it with repentant hearts. Jonah 3:10 says, "When God saw what they did and how they turned from their evil ways, he had compassion and did not bring upon them the destruction he had threatened" (NIV). God didn't remove Nineveh's sin; he forgave it. He no longer held their sin against them. Jonah was angered by God's compassion.

From our world's perspective, justice is served when people "get what they deserve." In fact, like Jonah, we often become angry when people are pardoned for their wrongdoing. Thankfully, God's view of justice differs from our own. Scripture tells us that we are all sinners, justified by faith in Jesus Christ to save us from the certain calamity that awaits us. We, like the Ninevites, are guilty of sin yet freed from the penalty we deserve so that we can live in fellowship with God. Justification is not getting away with our punishable acts, but being forgiven in spite of them.

## Connecting

Begin your group time with prayer. Pray Psalm 25:4–5 together: "Show me your ways, O LORD, teach me your paths; guide me in your truth and teach me, for you are God my Savior, and my hope is in you all day long" (NIV).

1. Pair up with your spiritual partner and turn to your *Personal Health Plan.* If you haven't established your spiritual partnership yet, do it now. (Refer to *Developing* in the *Leader's Notes* for *Session Two* for help.)

    Share with your partner any progress you have made toward accomplishing the goal you set for yourself for this study. What obstacles hinder you from following through? Make a note about your partner's progress and how you can pray for him or her.

2. All of us, at one time or another, have done something we shouldn't. As a child it could have been speaking disrespectfully to a parent. As an adult it might be speeding on the freeway or hurting someone in a relationship. Share an example of when you did something wrong but were forgiven. What did you feel in that moment? How do you feel about it today?

# Growing

Because of our flawed hearts, human beings are unable to earn God's acceptance, but we can be brought back into a relationship with God by being declared righteous (justified) through faith in Christ's sacrificial death on the cross. Through his sacrifice, we are freed from the penalty of sin.

Begin by reading Romans 3:21–31 aloud.

3. What does Paul say is the final goal of God's plan that is made possible through Jesus Christ?

    The Law of Moses told the Jews that when they sinned they should offer animal sacrifices to restore the people's relationship with God. The animal's blood was shed in place of the people's blood, to show them that sin was horrible and could not be ignored. No Jew thought sinless perfection was possible—that was the point of the animal sacrifices. Paul's radical claim is that Jesus took the place of all the animals that had ever been and would ever be sacrificed. He is the full and final *sacrifice of atonement* (2:25).

4. Many at the time of Paul's writing, and today, believe that righteousness comes through our actions. What argument does Paul make against this belief? See the *Study Notes* for a definition of righteousness.

5. The Jews in Jesus's day used Abraham as an example of being saved by keeping God's law of circumcision. But Paul says Abraham either earned his righteousness or received it as a free gift; it could not be both. What does Genesis 15:6, printed below, say about this?

Abram believed the LORD, and he credited it to him as righteousness. (NIV)

Now, read Romans 4 aloud, taking turns if desired.

6. For the Jews of Paul's day, Abraham was the quintessential Jew. So Paul looks at Abraham to support his argument that all are saved by faith in Jesus Christ. (See Rom. 4:9–12a.)

   God declared Abraham righteous on the basis of his faith alone, before he was circumcised. Why is this significant? See the *Study Notes* for more information on circumcision.

7. Paul expands Abraham's role as Father of the Jews (the circumcised), to encompass both the uncircumcised (Gentiles) and the circumcised (Jews). How is he able to do this according to Romans 4:12b–25?

Read Romans chapter 5.

8. What are some of the things that God gives to those who are justified by faith (Rom. 5:1–11)?

9. When you see all those benefits, how do you view God? See the *Study Notes* for more insight into justification.

10. Which of the following benefits of justification do you most need to focus on and become more aware of? Why that one?

   ☐ peace with God

   ☐ access to grace

   ☐ hope, perseverance, and joy amid suffering

   ☐ hope of ultimate glory in God's presence

   ☐ God's love poured into your heart

Justification, being declared righteous by God, comes as a gracious gift from God and is available only through faith, apart from anything we can do. Abraham's life proves that salvation comes through faith alone, because he was declared righteous on the basis of his faith even before he was circumcised. The benefits of our new "imputed" righteousness are peace with God, eternal life in his presence, and the ability to live with hope and joy now, no matter what life throws at us.

## Developing

In *Session One*, we discussed how God created each of us to serve him within the body of Christ. Romans 12:4–6 says: "Just as each of us has one body with many members, and these members do not all have the same function, so in Christ we who are many form one body, and each member belongs to all the others. We have different gifts, according to the grace given us" (NIV). Each of us has been given very special gifts for the purpose of filling specific needs within the body of Christ—the church.

11. Discuss some ways that we can serve the body of Christ. If you are already serving somewhere, share your experiences with the group.

    If you are not currently serving, is there a particular area of service that God has put on your heart to serve either this group or your local church? If not, pray about finding a ministry in which you can serve. As you take that first step, God will lead you to the ministry that expresses your passion.

12. On your *Personal Health Plan*, in the "Develop" section, answer the "WHERE are you serving?" question. If you are not currently serving, note one area where you will consider serving and commit to praying for the right opportunity and time to begin.

13. Romans 5:3–5 says: "Not only so, but we also rejoice in our sufferings, because we know that suffering produces perseverance; perseverance, character; and character, hope. And hope does not disappoint us, because God has poured out his love into our hearts by the Holy Spirit, whom he has given us" (NIV). Discuss the positive results of suffering found in these verses. Share how you have seen suffering produce these kinds of results in your life.

## Sharing

Matthew 5:16 says, "Let your light shine before men, that they may see your good deeds and praise your Father in heaven" (NIV). People are searching for purpose for living. As you live out God's purpose for your life, you become a visible reminder of God's design for others.

14. In the last session you wrote some names in the *Circles of Life* diagram. Have you followed up with those you identified who need to connect with other Christians? If not, when will you contact them?

    Go back to the *Circles of Life* diagram to remind yourself of the various people you come into contact with on a regular basis. Then commit to following through. Share your commitment with your spiritual partner and pray together for God to help you let his light shine through you.

15. If you have never invited Jesus to take control of your life, why not ask him in now? If you are not clear about God's gift of eternal life for everyone who believes in Jesus and how to receive this gift, take a minute to pray and ask God to help you understand what he wants you to do about trusting in Jesus.

## Surrendering

James 5:16 says: "Therefore confess your sins to each other and pray for each other so that you may be healed. The prayer of a righteous man is powerful and effective" (NIV).

16. Spend a few minutes sharing your praises and prayer requests. Record these on the *Prayer and Praise Report*. Then, pair up with your neighbor and spend time now praying for each other.

## Study Notes

*Righteousness:* Holy and upright living, in accordance with God's standard. God's character is the definition and source of all righteousness (Gen. 18:25; Deut. 32:4; Rom. 9:14). Therefore, human righteousness is defined in terms of God's.

*Circumcision:* In the New Testament devout Jews faithfully practiced circumcision as recognition of God's continuing covenant with Israel. But controversy over circumcision divided the early church (Eph. 2:11), which included believers from both Jewish and Gentile backgrounds. Gentile believers regarded their Jewish brethren as eccentric because of their dietary laws, Sabbath rules, and circumcision practices. Jewish believers tended to view their uncircumcised Gentile brothers as unenlightened and disobedient to the Law of Moses. Gentiles came to be regarded by the Jews as the "uncircumcision," a term of disrespect implying that non-Jewish peoples were outside the circle of God's love.

*Justification by Faith:* Although the Lord Jesus has paid the price for our justification, it is through our faith that he is received and his righteousness is experienced and enjoyed (Rom. 3:25–30). Faith is considered righteousness (Rom. 4:3, 9), not as human work (Rom. 4:5), but as the gift and work of God (John 6:28–29; Phil. 1:29).

## For Deeper Study (Optional)

Look up, read, and reflect on the following Scripture selections for further study on justification by faith alone.

- Acts 13:38–40
- Acts 15:6–11
- Galatians 2:15–16
- Galatians 3:10–14

- Galatians 3:23–25
- Titus 3:3–8

## Reflections

If you've been spending time each day connecting with God through his Word, congratulations! Some experts say that it takes twenty-one repetitions to develop a new habit. By the end of this week, you'll be well on your way to cultivating new spiritual habits that will encourage you in your walk with God. This week, continue to read the daily verses, giving prayerful consideration to what you learn about God, his Spirit, and his place in your life. Then, as before, record your thoughts, insights, or prayers in the space provided. On the sixth day, record a summary of what you have learned throughout the week.

*Day 1.* For all have sinned and fall short of the glory of God, and are justified freely by his grace through the redemption that came by Christ Jesus (Rom. 3:23–24 NIV).

REFLECT

_____

_____

_____

_____

*Day 2.* What does the Scripture say? "Abraham believed God, and it was credited to him as righteousness" (Rom. 4:3 NIV).

REFLECT

_____

_____

_____

_____

*Day 3.* Therefore, the promise comes by faith, so that it may be by grace and may be guaranteed to all Abraham's offspring—not only to those who are of the law but also to those who are of the faith of Abraham. He is the father of us all (Rom. 4:16 NIV).

REFLECT

_____

_____

_____

*Day 4.* Therefore, since we have been justified through faith, we have peace with God through our Lord Jesus Christ, through whom we have gained access by faith into this grace in which we now stand. And we rejoice in the hope of the glory of God (Rom. 5:1–2 NIV).

REFLECT

_____

_____

_____

*Day 5.* Consequently, just as the result of one trespass was condemnation for all men, so also the result of one act of righteousness was justification that brings life for all men (Rom. 5:18 NIV).

REFLECT

_____

_____

_____

_____

**Day 6.** Record your weekly summary of what God has shown you in the space below.

SUMMARY

_____

_____

_____

_____

# SANCTIFICATION
## LIVING OUT OUR LIFE OF RIGHTEOUSNESS

**Memory Verse: Therefore, there is now no condemnation for those who are in Christ Jesus, because through Christ Jesus the law of the Spirit of life set me free from the law of sin and death (Rom. 8:1–2 NIV).**

> Amazing grace, how sweet the sound
> That saved a wretch like me,
> I once was lost, but now am found,
> Was blind, but now I see.

From wretched slave-ship captain to Anglican clergyman and author of the timeless hymn "Amazing Grace," John Henry Newton's life is a striking portrayal of sanctification.

After a disgraceful desertion of the Royal Navy, Newton began his career in the Triangular Slave Trade. He said of himself, "I was capable of anything; I had not the least fear of God before my eyes, nor (so far as I remember) the least sensibility of conscience."[*]

After one violently stormy night at sea, Newton admitted his wretchedness and promised to change his life. He claimed to be a

---

[*] John Newton, *Out of the Depths* (Grand Rapids: Kregel Publications, 2003), 41.

"new man," yet many years passed before his conversion became evident in his daily life.

Newton once said of himself, "I am not what I might be, I am not what I ought to be, I am not what I wish to be, I am not what I hope to be. But I thank God I am not what I once was, and I can say with the great apostle, by the grace of God I am what I am." These words paint for us a true picture of sanctification.

Paul's words in Philippians 3:13–14 mirror this sentiment: "But one thing I do: Forgetting what is behind and straining toward what is ahead, I press on toward the goal to win the prize for which God has called me heavenward in Christ Jesus" (NIV). Becoming sanctified doesn't mean we're no longer sinners, it means we are sinners in the process of being transformed into the likeness of Jesus Christ.

## Connecting

Open your group with prayer. Thank God for what he has shown you during the last few weeks of your study of Romans and ask him to open the eyes of your heart that you might know him even better in the coming weeks.

1. Check in with your spiritual partner, or with another partner if yours is absent. Share something God taught you during your time in his Word this week, or read a brief section from your journal. What is one thing you discovered? Or, what obstacles hindered you from following through? Make a note about your partner's progress and how you can pray for him or her.

2. Share a time when you have resolved to make a life change. Were you successful? If so, to what do you attribute your success?

## Growing

Paul's focus in the first five chapters of Romans has been on humanity's need for reconciliation with God and what God has done to provide it. In chapters 6 through 8, Paul shifts to showing how we who have been reconciled with God live out our faith in Jesus Christ. One of the most intriguing questions of Christian faith is this: "How long does it take to be saved?" The answer is: "A moment, and a lifetime." Justification is the moment. Sanctification, or becoming more like Jesus Christ, is the lifetime. Our focus in this session will be on the process of sanctification.

Please read Romans chapter 6 aloud.

3. Paul speaks in Romans 6:1–14 of the spiritual reality that baptism represents—what happens to each of us when we identify with Christ's death and resurrection. How does identifying with Christ's death and resurrection affect our relationship to sin?

4. Dying to sin doesn't mean sin no longer tempts us. It means sin no longer owns us. What difference does that make to us in practice? What is it like to be a slave of sin? Give some examples.

5. Paul writes: "Count yourselves dead to sin but alive to God in Christ Jesus. Therefore do not let sin reign in your mortal body so that you obey its evil desires. Do not offer the parts of your body to sin, as instruments of wickedness, but rather offer yourselves to God, as those who have been brought from death to life; and offer the parts of your body to him as instruments of righteousness" (6:11–13 NIV).

    In practical terms, how does a person go about behaving as one dead to sin but alive to God? How does she refuse to let sin reign in her? How does he offer the parts of his body to God as instruments of righteousness?

6. Read Romans 6:15–23. Why isn't it an option for a person to cling to a few favorite sins but still belong to Christ? What are the benefits of being slaves of righteousness? The idea of being "slaves" of righteousness is deliberately shocking. How do you respond to that imagery?

In Romans 7, Paul explains how the Law of Moses fits into this picture of death and resurrection. Just as we are dead to sin, we are also dead to the law. Keeping the Law of Moses isn't a viable route to holiness, because the law is powerless to enable us to keep it. Chapter 7 sets up the solution Paul lays out in chapter 8: The Holy Spirit empowers the obedience and holiness that the law is powerless to do. The law can only convict us of our wrongdoing; it can't enable us to do right. But the Spirit can, if we let him.

7. Romans 7:14–24 describes the frustrating situation of someone trying to keep the Law of Moses without the sacrifice of Christ and the aid of the Holy Spirit. What is frustrating about that experience?

Read Romans chapter 8.

8. In Romans 8:1–8, Paul contrasts life in the flesh (or, life in the "sinful nature") with life in the Spirit. Life in the flesh is life lived by one's own will, ignoring God. How does Paul describe life in the Spirit? What is the end result of life in the flesh? What are the benefits of life in the Spirit, according to 8:1–11?

9. To have faith in Christ means to reject life in the flesh and choose life in the Spirit. Believing in Christ but rejecting the Spirit isn't an option in Paul's mind. It's both Christ and the Spirit, or neither. As believers, we have the obligation and the privilege to put to death the misdeeds of the body by the power of the Spirit (8:12–13; see also 8:26–30). How does that work in practice? How is it different from just trying hard? How is it different from sitting around waiting for the Spirit to magically change us?

10. The Spirit of God is at work in our lives now, and will continue to be at work in our lives in the future. What is the future work of the Spirit (Rom. 8:14–27)? See the *Study Notes* for insight into sanctification.

11. What encouragement does Paul offer in 8:18–39 for us to be joyful and confident even when life in the Spirit is challenging?

## Developing

Last week we talked about using our God-given gifts to serve him in the body of Christ. First Peter 4:10 says: "Each one should use whatever gift he has received to serve others, faithfully administering God's grace in its various forms" (NIV).

12. The Bible reveals the many spiritual gifts given to believers. Take five minutes and review the *Spiritual Gifts Inventory* in the *Appendix*. Discuss which of the listed gifts you believe you may have.

   Once you have an idea about what your spiritual gifts are, discuss how you may be able to use them in ministry. Plan to investigate the opportunities available to you in your church and get involved in serving the body of Christ. It's amazing to experience God using you to fill a specific need within his church.

## Sharing

The Lord enables us through the power of his Holy Spirit to share Jesus boldly and without hindrance as Acts 4:31 says: "After they prayed, the place where they were meeting was shaken. And they were all filled with the Holy Spirit and spoke the word of God boldly" (NIV).

13. In *Session Two*, you identified people within your *Circles of Life* that needed connection to Christian community. Jesus's commission in Acts 1:8 included sharing him not only within our own circles of influence (our Jerusalem), but also in Judea and Samaria and the ends of the earth. Judea included the region in which Jerusalem was located. Today, this might include neighboring communities or cities. As a group, discuss

the following possible actions you can take to share Jesus with your Judea in a tangible way. Here are a few ideas:

☐ Collect new blankets and/or socks for the homeless. Bring them with you next week and have someone deliver them to a ministry serving the homeless in a nearby city.

☐ Bring nonperishable food items to group next week and designate one person to donate them to a local food bank.

☐ As a group, pick a night to volunteer to serve meals at a downtown mission or homeless shelter.

14. On your *Personal Health Plan*, in the "Sharing" section, answer the "WHEN are you shepherding another person in Christ?" question.

## Surrendering

First John 3:11 says: "This is the message you heard from the beginning: We should love one another" (NIV). One way to show your love for one another is to pray focused prayer over each other's needs.

## Study Notes

*Sanctification:* The process of God's grace by which the believer is separated from sin and becomes dedicated to God's righteousness. Accomplished by the Word of God (John 17:7–8) and the Holy Spirit (Rom. 8:3–4), sanctification results in holiness, or purification from the guilt and power of sin.

## For Deeper Study [Optional]

Sanctification is a process and requires our cooperation with the Father, the Son, and the Holy Spirit. See how each of these is involved in the sanctification of the believer according to the following Scriptures:

### The Believer
- Leviticus 11:44–45
- Romans 6:19
- 1 Peter 1:15–16

### God the Father
- Exodus 31:13
- Leviticus 20:7–8
- Jude 24–25

### God the Son
- Hebrews 2:10–12

### God the Holy Spirit
- 2 Thessalonians 2:13–14
- 1 Peter 1:2

## Reflections

Second Timothy 3:16–17 reads: "All Scripture is God-breathed and is useful for teaching, rebuking, correcting and training in righteousness, so that the man of God may be thoroughly equipped for every good work" (NIV). Allow God's Word to train you in righteousness as you read, reflect on, and respond to the Scripture in your daily time with God this week.

**Day 1.** What shall we say, then? Shall we go on sinning so that grace may increase? By no means! We died to sin; how can we live in it any longer? (Rom. 6:1 NIV).

REFLECT

_____

_____

_____

_____

**Day 2.** In the same way, count yourselves dead to sin but alive to God in Christ Jesus. Therefore do not let sin reign in your mortal body so that you obey its evil desires (Rom. 6:11–12 NIV).

REFLECT

_____

_____

_____

_____

**Day 3.** What a wretched man I am! Who will rescue me from this body of death? Thanks be to God—through Jesus Christ our Lord! (Rom. 7:24–25a NIV).

REFLECT

_____

_____

_____

_____

**Day 4.** Therefore, there is now no condemnation for those who are in Christ Jesus, because through Christ Jesus the law of the Spirit of life set me free from the law of sin and death (Rom. 8:1–2 NIV).

REFLECT

_____

_____

_____

_____

*Day 5.* For I am convinced that neither death nor life, neither angels nor demons, neither the present nor the future, nor any powers, neither height nor depth, nor anything else in all creation, will be able to separate us from the love of God that is in Christ Jesus our Lord (Rom. 8:38–39 NIV).

REFLECT

_____

_____

_____

_____

*Day 6.* Use the following space to record your summary of how God has challenged you this week.

SUMMARY

_____

_____

_____

_____

# GOD'S PLAN FOR HIS CHOSEN PEOPLE ISRAEL

**Memory Verse:** If you confess with your mouth, "Jesus is Lord," and believe in your heart that God raised him from the dead, you will be saved. For it is with your heart that you believe and are justified, and it is with your mouth that you confess and are saved (Rom. 10:9–10 NIV).

A covenant is not just a promise; it is a binding agreement that a promised action will take place. One example of a covenant is marriage. A man and a woman make a promise to love one another for better, for worse, for richer, for poorer, in sickness, or in health, until parted by death. This covenant promise is witnessed, bound, and protected by the law.

When God entered into a covenant with the nation of Israel, it was a binding agreement. To this very day, although Israel rejected God, God has not rejected Israel. He remains faithful to his covenant promises and will restore them if they return to him in faith.

## Connecting

Begin your time together by offering a prayer of thanksgiving for all God has already done in your small group during this study.

1. Check in with your spiritual partner, or with another partner if yours is absent. Talk about any challenges you are currently facing in reaching the goals you have set throughout this study. Tell your spiritual partner how he or she has helped you follow through with each step. Be sure to write down your partner's progress.

2. Frequently, we ignore good advice or instruction. It could be something simple like ignoring the assembly instructions for a new piece of furniture; or it could be something more serious like ignoring the warning light on our automobile dashboard. When have you ignored good advice or instruction in your life and what was the result?

## Growing

After leaving the subject for several chapters, Paul comes back to the subject of the Jewish people, whom he calls Israel, in Romans 9–11. Paul longs for the salvation of his Jewish kinsmen. He speaks of his deep love for them. He has demonstrated his commitment to them in his ministry. In every city Paul entered, he went first to Jews to proclaim the good news of Jesus Christ. Throughout his life, Paul never let go of his desire to see Israel accept God's plan of salvation. Begin by reading Romans 9:1–29.

3. God promised Abraham that his offspring would be God's chosen people, yet from the beginning God's favor was toward those he chose, and not every physical descendant of Abraham was automatically chosen. What do we learn about God's right to choose one person and not another in Romans 9:6–13? See the *Study Notes* for insights.

4. Many accuse God of being unjust when he chooses some and not others (Rom. 9:10–13). How should we understand God's choice of Jacob over Esau in Romans 9:13–16? Is this an example of injustice? If so, how? If not, of what is it an example?

5. Now, read Romans 9:17–29. Paul goes even further with his explanation of God's sovereignty when he speaks of God hardening who he wants to harden (9:18). How does this example extend God's sovereignty?

6. Paul doesn't think it's unfair for God to harden someone like Pharaoh. Why not?

Read Romans 9:30–10:21.

7. According to Paul (Rom. 9:30–33), the Israel of his generation was losing out on salvation because they were still trying to be righteous by keeping the Law of Moses instead of accepting Jesus as the Messiah—the promised king and the final sacrifice of atonement. They were still sacrificing animals in the temple, according to the Law of Moses, refusing to believe that Jesus had put an end to all that. Even today, Jews have a hard time accepting that the crucified Jesus is the one their Scriptures foretold. How does Paul describe his complex thoughts and feelings about his fellow Jews in 10:1–4, 21? Why would it be hard for a Jew, whose family has been living according to the Law of Moses for centuries, to accept that someone crucified as a criminal is Israel's prophesied king, and that keeping the law is no longer necessary?

Read Romans chapter 11, taking turns if desired.

8. Paul says that he is living proof that God has not rejected his people Israel. Paul, a descendant of Abraham and a member of the tribe of Benjamin, is an example of the remnant of Israel discussed in Romans 11:1–5. What does this suggest about God's plan for the Jews? See the *Study Notes* for insight into the remnant of Israel.

9. God's plan for Israel, revealed in his covenant with Abraham (Gen. 12), was for Israel to be a blessing to all the nations. What positive result has come from Israel's rejection of Christ (Rom. 11:11–12)?

10. According to 11:13–24, why do Gentile Christians have no excuse for looking down on Jews?

In spite of Israel's history of rejection and hardened hearts, Paul does not give up hope for their salvation. As he speaks about a remnant of believers among the Jews, including himself, he is careful to distinguish between an ethnic group and individual people. His hope for the future is that many Jews will come to faith in Jesus Christ and be saved with him.

11. How does Romans 9–11 affect your view of God? Of the Jews?

## Developing

By this point in the study, hopefully you've developed some new growth disciplines such as accountability, Scripture memorization, meditation on the Word of God, and prayer. Consider taking your commitment to know God better one step further.

12. If you've been spending time with God each day, consider journaling as a way to grow even closer to God. Read through *Journaling 101* found in the *Appendix*. Commit this week to spending a portion of your time with God journaling.

13. Briefly discuss the future of your group. How many of you are willing to stay together as a group and work through another study together? If you have time, turn to the *Small Group Agreement* and talk about any changes you would like to make as you move forward as a group.

## Sharing

Jesus's final command to his disciples was to "be [his] witnesses in Jerusalem, and in all Judea and Samaria, and to the ends of the earth" (Acts 1:8 NIV). Jesus wanted his disciples to share his Gospel not only with their local communities, but also the world. You can be involved in taking the Gospel to all nations too.

14. Prayerfully consider the following actions as a first step toward fulfilling Jesus's commission in your life.

   ☐ Hang a world map in the place where you pray at home. Pray for the world, then each continent, and then each country, as the Lord leads you. Or, consider praying for the countries printed on your clothing labels as you get dressed every day.

   ☐ Send financial support to a missionary in a foreign country or a world mission's organization.

   ☐ Sponsor a child through a Christ-centered humanitarian aid organization.

15. Last week you discussed one tangible way to share Jesus in your "Judea and Samaria." If you brought items to donate tonight. Spend a few minutes praying for the individuals or families that will receive them.

## Surrendering

Philippians 4:6 tells us: "Do not be anxious about anything, but in everything, by prayer and petition, with thanksgiving, present your requests to God" (NIV). Prayer represents a powerful act of surrender to the Lord as we put aside our pride and lay our burdens at his feet.

## Study Notes

*Covenant:* The concept of covenant between God and his people is one of the most important theological truths of the Bible. By making a covenant with Abraham, God promised to bless his descendants and to make them his special people. Abraham, in return, was to remain faithful to God and to serve as a channel through which God's blessings could flow to the rest of the world (Gen. 12:1–3).

*God's Chosen People:* A name for the Hebrew people, whom God chose as his special instruments. As a holy people set apart to worship God, they were to make his name known throughout the earth (Deut. 7:6, 7; Ps. 105:43). In the New Testament, Peter describes Christians as members of a "chosen generation" (1 Peter 2:9 NKJV).

*Isaac:* Abraham had two sons: Ishmael and Isaac. God chose to work out his promise through the line of Isaac, not Ishmael. Likewise, Isaac had two sons, and God chose to pass the promise through the line of Isaac's son Jacob, not Esau.

*Remnant of Israel:* A remnant is something left over. Despite widespread apostasy (abandonment of the faith), a faithful remnant of Jews remained.

## For Deeper Study [Optional]

In our study of Romans today, Paul quoted from many Old Testament Scriptures to communicate God's sovereign plan for his chosen people. Listed below are some of the high points addressed by Paul in this selection. Read and reflect on each of these. How does God's faithfulness to his Word provide hope in the eventual salvation of Israel?

- Genesis 12:1–3—God's promise to Abraham
- Genesis 27:1–40—God chooses some over others

- Exodus 9:13–19—God chooses some for good and some for evil in working out his sovereign plan.
- Isaiah 6:8–10—God hardens who he wants to harden
- Isaiah 65:1–12—Israel is disobedient and stubborn and loses out on salvation
- Isaiah 59:20–21—Israel will be saved

## Reflections

The Lord promised Joshua success and prosperity in Joshua 1:8 when he said: "Do not let this Book of the Law depart from your mouth; meditate on it day and night, so that you may be careful to do everything written in it. Then you will be prosperous and successful" (NIV). We too can claim this promise for our lives as we commit to meditate on the Word of God each day. As in previous weeks, read and meditate on the daily verses and record any prayers or insights you gain in the space provided. Summarize what you have learned this week on Day 6.

*Day 1.* What then shall we say? Is God unjust? Not at all! For he says to Moses, "I will have mercy on whom I have mercy, and I will have compassion on whom I have compassion" (Rom. 9:14–15 NIV).

REFLECT

_____

_____

_____

_____

*Day 2.* If you confess with your mouth, "Jesus is Lord," and believe in your heart that God raised him from the dead, you will be saved. For it is with your heart that you believe and are justified, and it is with your mouth that you confess and are saved (Rom. 10:9–10 NIV).

REFLECT

_____

_____

_____

_____

*Day 3.* For there is no difference between Jew and Gentile—the same Lord is Lord of all and richly blesses all who call on him, for, "Everyone who calls on the name of the Lord will be saved" (Rom. 10:12–13 NIV).

REFLECT

_____

_____

_____

_____

*Day 4.* So too, at the present time there is a remnant chosen by grace. And if by grace, then it is no longer by works; if it were, grace would no longer be grace (Rom. 11:5–6 NIV).

REFLECT

_____

_____

_____

_____

**Day 5.** Oh, the depth of the riches of the wisdom and knowledge of God! How unsearchable his judgments, and his paths beyond tracing out! "Who has known the mind of the Lord? Or who has been his counselor?" "Who has ever given to God, that God should repay him?" For from him and through him and to him are all things. To him be the glory forever! Amen (Rom. 11:33–36 NIV).

REFLECT

_____

_____

_____

_____

**Day 6.** Use the following space to write any thoughts God has put in your heart and mind during _Session Five_ and your _Reflections_ time this week.

SUMMARY

_____

_____

_____

_____

# LIVING OUT THIS NEW LIFE, PART 1

Memory Verse: Do not conform any longer to the pattern of this world, but be transformed by the renewing of your mind. Then you will be able to test and approve what God's will is—his good, pleasing and perfect will (Rom. 12:2 NIV).

Shadrach, Meshach, and Abednego faced the ultimate test—living out the faith they professed in the heat of adversity. The king, Nebuchadnezzar had issued a decree that everyone should bow down and worship a massive golden idol erected in his own honor. Anyone who didn't would immediately be thrown into a blazing furnace.

In spite of the fact that everyone around them fell down and worshiped the image, Shadrach, Meshach, and Abednego refused. In fact, they didn't pay any attention to Nebuchadnezzar at all. When questioned by the king, they declared: "We do not need to defend ourselves before you in this matter. If we are thrown into the blazing furnace, the God we serve is able to save us from it, and he will rescue us from your hand, O king. But even if he does not, we want you to know, O king, that we will not serve your gods or worship the image of gold you have set up" (Dan. 3:16–18 NIV).

If you're familiar with the story, you know that God delivered them from their trial. Shadrach, Meshach, and Abednego were able to stand up against the pressure to conform and boldly proclaim their faith in God. As a result, God blessed their lives.

Many Christians choose to live their "church lives" on Sunday while living "worldly lives" the remainder of the week, but the Bible tells us to no longer conform to the pattern of this world and renew our minds to the point that our thoughts and behaviors are transformed into godly living. As we choose to live according to God's pattern for our lives we will become stronger Christians able to discern the will of the Lord and able to live holy and pleasing lives in spite of what the world brings our way.

## Connecting

Begin your discussion time with prayer. Thank the Lord for any new insight you've received as you've studied the book of Romans. Ask him to make you receptive to what he has for you today.

1. Check in with your spiritual partner, or with another partner if yours is absent. Share your progress and any challenges you are currently facing. Take a few minutes to pray for each other now. Be sure to write down your partner's progress.

2. Think about teams—sports teams, leadership teams, serving teams, work teams, and "home" teams. What are some common challenges teams face as they bring together different kinds of people to work toward a common goal?

## Growing

In chapter 12, Paul's discussion of humanity's problem of sin and how we as sinners can be restored to a right relationship with God is completed. From this point forward in Romans, Paul moves to the practical elements of our relationship with God.

Please read Romans chapter 12 aloud.

Paul's has explained humanity's problem of sin and how sinners can be restored to a right relationship with God. From this point

forward in Romans, Paul describes in practical terms what life by faith in Christ, in the power of the Holy Spirit, looks like.
Please read Romans 12 aloud.

3. At the top of Paul's agenda for a life transformed by God's Spirit are: 1) offer your body and 2) pursue the renewal of your mind (12:1–2). What is one way of offering your body to God's service? Why is the renewal of your mind essential?

4. Give some examples of ways we are influenced by the world's values and behaviors (12:2). How can we move away from the world's values and behaviors toward God's values?

5. Some describe spiritual transformation as taking off the clothing of the world and putting on the clothing of God. What kinds of things need to be "put off" and "put on" if we are to be transformed?

6. One aspect of doing God's will is serving the body of Christ. When we serve, exercising our gifts for the good of the Church, what should our attitude be (Rom. 12:3–8)? Why is attitude so vital?

7. God has adopted us into a new family—his Church. Just as in a family, everyone in the Church has roles and responsibilities. What are some of those roles and responsibilities mentioned in Romans 12:6–8?

8. Some of the most significant challenges in our lives are relationships—in our marriages, families, workplaces, and even small groups. Read Romans 12:9–21. Choose one of these instructions for healthy relationships and talk about how it would make a difference in one of your relationships.

9. Romans 12:19–21 (NIV) says: "Do not take revenge, my friends, but leave room for God's wrath, for it is written: 'It is mine to avenge; I will repay,' says the Lord. On the contrary: 'If your enemy is hungry, feed him; if he is thirsty, give him something

to drink. In doing this, you will heap burning coals on his head.' Do not be overcome by evil, but overcome evil with good." The idea of repaying evil with good seems counterintuitive. How does God model this for us in his relationship with us?

The appropriate response to God's great gift of salvation is to give ourselves completely to him and live lives worthy of our new position in Christ.

## Developing

Jesus lived his life in service to God and others. In John 13:15, Jesus instructed his apostles to follow his example saying: "I have set you an example that you should do as I have done for you" (NIV). Not only did Jesus tell us to serve one another, he empowered us with the gifts of the Holy Spirit. Embrace your gifts and learn to serve as the Holy Spirit leads you.

10. Paul provides us with a partial list of spiritual gifts in Romans 12:6–8. During previous weeks, we've discussed these and other spiritual gifts as listed on the *Spiritual Gifts Inventory*. Take a few minutes now to review them again. If you haven't already, share what you believe your spiritual gift(s) are. If you are already serving, share where you have found opportunities to exercise your gift(s), either within the small group or in your church. If you still do not know what your spiritual gift(s) are, you can review the inventory with a trusted friend who knows you well. Chances are they have witnessed one or more of these gifts in your life.

11. During *Session Two*, you should have discussed whether your group would like to have a potluck or social. Take a few minutes now to tie up any loose ends in your plan.

## Sharing

Philippians 2:3–4 says: "Do nothing out of selfish ambition or vain conceit, but in humility consider others better than yourselves. Each of you should look not only to your own interests, but also to the interests of others" (NIV). Humility and sympathy are the cornerstones of our relationships with others; especially those with whom we hope to share Jesus.

12. Discuss how you can visibly demonstrate humility and sympathy in your relationships. Is there a person that comes to mind who needs your sympathy? Write their name below and look for an opportunity to practice the characteristics of humility and sympathy in your relationship with them this week. Share your decision with your spiritual partner for encouragement and prayer support.

    Name _____

## Surrendering

God has given each of us the opportunity to live out our Christian lives daily in our world. Not only that, but he has also given us everything we need to live like Christ through the power of the Holy Spirit.

13. Spend a minute thanking God for all he has given us to live like Christ in our relationships within the body of Christ and in the world.

14. Turn to the *Personal Health Plan* and individually consider the "HOW are you surrendering your heart?" question. Look to the *Sample Personal Health Plan* for help. Share some of your thoughts in the group.

15. Share your praises and prayer requests with one another. Record these on the *Prayer and Praise Report.* Then pray together with your one other person in your group.

## For Deeper Study (Optional)

Today, we talked about how God models the principle of repaying evil with good. Have you thought of returning evil with good? Reflect on and pray about whether your life needs a new strategy for overcoming evil? Where could you put your new strategy to work this week? Record your thoughts below.

_____

_____

_____

_____

## Reflections

J. Hudson Taylor once said, "Do not have your concert first, and then tune your instruments afterwards. Begin the day with the Word of God and prayer, and get first of all into harmony with Him."* Get into harmony with God as you spend time with him this week. Read and reflect on the daily verses. Then record your thoughts, insights, or prayers in the *Reflect* sections that follow. On the sixth day record your summary of what God has taught you this week.

* Charlie Jones and Bob Kelly, *The Tremendous Power of Prayer: A Collection of Quotes and InspirationalThoughts to Inspire Your Prayer Life* (West Monroe, LA: Howard Books, 2000).

*Day 1.* For by the grace given me I say to every one of you: Do not think of yourself more highly than you ought, but rather think of yourself with sober judgment, in accordance with the measure of faith God has given you. Just as each of us has one body with many members, and these members do not all have the same function (Rom. 12:3–4 NIV).

REFLECT

_____

_____

_____

_____

*Day 2.* We have different gifts, according to the grace given us. If a man's gift is prophesying, let him use it in proportion to his faith. If it is serving, let him serve; if it is teaching, let him teach; if it is encouraging, let him encourage; if it is contributing to the needs of others, let him give generously; if it is leadership, let him govern diligently; if it is showing mercy, let him do it cheerfully (Rom. 12:6–8 NIV).

REFLECT

_____

_____

_____

_____

*Day 3.* Love must be sincere. Hate what is evil; cling to what is good. Be devoted to one another in brotherly love. Honor one another above yourselves (Rom. 12:9–10 NIV).

REFLECT

_____

_____

_____

_____

*Day 4.* Bless those who persecute you; bless and do not curse. Rejoice with those who rejoice; mourn with those who mourn. Live in harmony with one another (Rom. 12:14–16 NIV).

REFLECT

_____

_____

_____

_____

*Day 5.* Do not repay anyone evil for evil. Be careful to do what is right in the eyes of everybody. If it is possible, as far as it depends on you, live at peace with everyone (Rom. 12:17–18 NIV).

REFLECT

_____

_____

_____

_____

*Day 6.* Record your summary of what God has taught you this week.

SUMMARY

_____

_____

_____

_____

# LIVING OUT THIS NEW LIFE, PART 2

Memory Verse: Therefore, I urge you, brothers, in view of God's mercy, to offer your bodies as living sacrifices, holy and pleasing to God—this is your spiritual act of worship (Rom. 12:1 NIV).

Jason Upton wrote and recorded a beautiful song entitled "No Sacrifice," which truly communicates the heart of Romans 12:1. It goes like this:

> To You I give my life, not just the parts I want to
> To You I sacrifice these dreams that I hold onto
> To You I give the gifts Your love has given me
> How can I hoard the treasures that You designed for free
> To You I give my future as long as it may last
> To You I give my present
> To You I give my past

The chorus goes on to say, "Your thoughts are higher than mine; Your words are deeper than mine; Your love is stronger than mine; this is no sacrifice; here's my life."

Everything that we call ours is because of God. He blessed us with everything we need when he offered his Son as atonement for our sins. Our response to being justified through God's amazing grace

71

and mercy should be living lives of daily sacrifice, offering to him everything that is ours to give.

## Connecting

Begin this final session with prayer, specifically thanking God for how he has challenged and encouraged you during this study.

1. Take time in this final session to connect with your spiritual partner. What has God been showing you through these sessions about justification and sanctification? Check in with each other about the progress you have made in your spiritual growth during this study and make plans about whether you will continue in your mentoring relationship outside your Bible study group.

2. Share with the group one thing that you learned about God through this study that has encouraged you. Also, if you have questions about Romans or Christian doctrine as a result of this study, discuss where you might find the answers.

## Growing

In Romans 13–16, Paul continues to describe how to live by faith in the power of the Spirit. The subjects he chooses are wide ranging—including everything from our relationship to civil authorities, to paying taxes; from the promise of Christ's imminent return, to eating and drinking; and from Paul's past ministry, to his future ministry. All of this instruction explains how to live out new life in Jesus Christ. Begin by reading Romans 13 aloud.

3. What does it mean to submit to governing authorities (13:1–5)? Just a few years after Paul wrote this letter, the Roman government falsely accused Christians in Rome of arson. It executed hundreds of Christians who refused to renounce their faith and offer incense to the emperor as a god. Do you think their

refusal violated Paul's instruction to submit? Why or why not?

Some ethical choices, like loving one's neighbor, are right always and for everyone (13:8–10). Some choices, like coveting someone else's property, are wrong always and for everyone (13:9, 13–14). But there are also what Paul calls "disputable matters" (14:1), things like whether it's okay to eat meat or drink wine, that Christians legitimately disagree about.

Read Romans 14:1–15:13.

4. What principles do you find in 14:1–15:4 to help Christians deal with disagreements over disputable matters?

5. The Holy Spirit gives us vast areas of freedom, but our freedom is limited by love (13:8), building others up rather than tearing them down (14:19–21), seeking righteousness, peace, and joy (14:17), and remembering that we will have to give an account to God for our actions (14:10–12). Do you think we can trust Christians to be guided by the Holy Spirit and biblical principles like these, or do you think churches should make rules about disputable matters so that people don't fall into sin? Please explain your view.

6. Joe is a Christian. He wants to play poker and have a beer once a week with his non-Christian co-workers. He says it's an opportunity for evangelism. His Christian friends are uncomfortable with his doing that. How can Joe and his friends apply Paul's principles to this situation?

7. How would Paul want you to deal with disagreements in your group?

Now read Romans 15:14–16:27.

8. As he comes to a close, Paul shares about his past ministry to the Gentiles, his present ministry of delivering an offering from the new Gentile churches to the needy in Jerusalem, and

his future plans to visit Rome on his way to Spain. How does Paul communicate his passion for ministry in 15:14–33?

9. Chapter 16 is highly personal. What do we learn about the early church from these verses?

Why do you think Paul warns against divisions in the church in 16:17–19?

10. Paul's final words in the letter are found in 16:25–27. How would you put this praise into your own words?

To live worthy of our new position in Christ we must submit to every human authority, pay every debt we owe, focus on love, avoid judging one another, and instead seek to build each other up. Paul's ministry is a model for this as he seeks to expand his ministry to the Gentiles through his relationship with the Roman church.

## Developing

Romans 12:1 tells us: "Therefore, I urge you, brothers, in view of God's mercy, to offer your bodies as living sacrifices, holy and pleasing to God—this is your spiritual act of worship" (NIV). Living this type of sacrificial life that is pleasing to God requires that we offer our lives to him every day, living each day with the Lord and his Word always before us.

11. Discuss some practical ways that you can live your day-to-day life as a living sacrifice to the Lord.

12. "'Son of man, eat this scroll I am giving you and fill your stomach with it.' So I ate it, and it tasted as sweet as honey in my mouth" (Ezek. 3:3 NIV). This week as we wrap up our study, recommit to spending regular time eating God's scroll, the Bible. Don't just give it a casual glance or rush to get through a Bible reading plan, but really chew it up, digest it, and allow every word to nourish you. Not only will you find

that it strengthens your faith, but as it is absorbed deep into your hearts, you will find it sweetens your lives.

13. If your group still needs to make decisions about continuing to meet after this session, have that discussion now. Talk about what you will study, who will lead, and where and when you will meet.

    Review your *Small Group Agreement* and evaluate how well you met your goals. Discuss any changes you want to make as you move forward. As your group starts a new study this is a great time to take on a new role or change roles of service in your group. What new role will you take on? If you are uncertain, maybe your group members have some ideas for you. Remember you aren't making a lifetime commitment to the new role; it will only be for a few weeks. Maybe someone would like to share a role with you if you don't feel ready to serve solo.

## Sharing

First Peter 3:15 says: "But in your hearts set apart Christ as Lord. Always be prepared to give an answer to everyone who asks you to give the reason for the hope that you have" (NIV). As this Scripture tells us, we should always be prepared to give an answer for the hope that we have found in Christ.

14. During the course of this study, you have made many commitments to share Jesus with the people in your life, either by inviting your friends to grow in Christian community or by sharing the Gospel in words or actions with unbelievers. Share with the group any highlights that you experienced as you stepped out in faith to share with others.

15. Our memory verse this week (Rom. 12:1) tells us that love of others is the fulfillment of the law. Is there a personal relationship in your life that could be improved if you were to love that

person as yourself? What specific ways could you demonstrate love and kindness towards that person this week?

Name: _____

Plan of Action: _____

### Surrendering

16. Take a couple of minutes to review the praises you have recorded over the past five weeks on the *Prayer and Praise Report*. Close by praying for your prayer requests and thanking God for what he's done in your group during this study.

## Reflections

As you read through this final week of *Reflections*, prayerfully consider what God is showing you about his character, the Holy Spirit, and how he wants you to grow and change. Then, write down your thoughts or prayers in the space provided. Don't let this concluding week of *Reflections* be your last. Commit to continue reading, reflecting, and meditating on the Word of God daily. Use Day 6 to record your prayer of commitment to see this discipline become habit.

*Day 1.* For none of us lives to himself alone and none of us dies to himself alone. If we live, we live to the Lord; and if we die, we die to the Lord. So, whether we live or die, we belong to the Lord (Rom. 14:7–8 NIV).

REFLECT

_____

_____

_____

_____

*Day 2.* It is written: "As surely as I live," says the Lord, "every knee will bow before me; every tongue will confess to God." So then, each of us will give an account of himself to God (Rom. 14:11–12 NIV).

REFLECT

_____

_____

_____

_____

*Day 3.* May the God who gives endurance and encouragement give you a spirit of unity among yourselves as you follow Christ Jesus, so that with one heart and mouth you may glorify the God and Father of our Lord Jesus Christ (Rom. 15:5 NIV).

REFLECT

_____

_____

_____

_____

*Day 4.* I urge you, brothers, to watch out for those who cause divisions and put obstacles in your way that are contrary to the teaching you have learned. Keep away from them (Rom. 16:17 NIV).

REFLECT

_____

_____

_____

_____

**Day 5.** Now to him who is able to establish you by my gospel and the proclamation of Jesus Christ, according to the revelation of the mystery hidden for long ages past, but now revealed and made known through the prophetic writings by the command of the eternal God, so that all nations might believe and obey him—to the only wise God be glory forever through Jesus Christ! Amen (Rom. 16:25–27 NIV).

REFLECT

_____

_____

_____

_____

**Day 6.** Use the following space to write your prayer of commitment to continue spending time daily in God's Word and prayer.

SUMMARY

_____

_____

_____

_____

# FREQUENTLY ASKED QUESTIONS

### What do we do on the first night of our group?

Like all fun things in life—have a party! A "get to know you" coffee, dinner, or dessert is a great way to launch a new study. You may want to review the *Small Group Agreement* and share the names of a few friends you can invite to join you. But most importantly, have fun before your study time begins.

### Where do we find new members for our group?

This can be challenging, especially for new groups that have only a few people or for existing groups that lose a few people along the way. We encourage you to pray with your group and then brainstorm a list of people from work, church, your neighborhood, your children's school, family, the gym, and so forth. Then have each group member invite several of the people on his or her list. Another good strategy is to ask church leaders to make an announcement that your group is open to new members.

No matter how you find members, it's vital that you stay on the lookout for new people to join your group. All groups tend to go through healthy attrition—the result of moves, releasing new leaders, ministry opportunities, and so forth—and if the group gets too small, it could be at risk of shutting down. If you and your group stay open, you'll be amazed at the people God sends your way. The next person just might become a friend for life. You never know!

### How long will this group meet?

It's totally up to the group—once you come to the end of this study. Most groups meet weekly for at least their first six months together, but every other week can work as well. We strongly recommend that the group meet for the first six months on a weekly basis if at all possible. This allows for continuity, and if people miss a meeting they aren't gone for a whole month.

At the end of this study, each group member may decide whether he or she wants to continue on for another study. Some groups launch relationships that last for years, and others are stepping-stones into another group experience. Either way, enjoy the journey.

### What if this group is not working for me?

Personality conflicts, life stage differences, geographical distance, level of spiritual maturity, or any number of things can cause you to feel the group doesn't work for you. Relax. Pray for God's direction, and at the end of this study decide whether to continue with this group or find another. You don't buy the first car you look at or marry the first person you date, and the same goes with a group. Don't bail out before the study is finished—God might have something to teach you. Also, don't run from conflict or prejudge people before you have given them a chance. God is still working in you too!

### Who is the leader?

Most groups have an official leader. But ideally, the group will mature and members will share the facilitation of meetings. We have discovered that healthy groups share hosting and leading of the group. This model ensures that all members grow, give their unique contribution, and develop their gifts. This study guide and the Holy Spirit can keep things on track even when you share leadership. Christ has promised to be in your midst as you gather. Ultimately, God is your leader each step of the way.

## How do we handle the child care needs in our group?

This can be a sensitive issue. We suggest that you empower the group to openly brainstorm solutions. You may try one option that works for a while and then adjust over time. Our favorite approach is for adults to meet in the living room or dining room, and share the cost of a babysitter (or two) who can be with the kids in a different part of the house. In this way, parents don't have to be away from their children all evening when their children are too young to be left at home. A second option is to use one home for the kids and a second home (close by) for the adults. A third idea is to rotate the responsibility of providing a lesson or care for the children either in the same home or in another home nearby. This can be an incredible blessing for kids. Finally, the most common idea is to decide that you need to have a night to invest in your spiritual lives individually or as a couple, and make your own arrangements for child care. No matter what decision the group makes, the best approach is to dialogue openly about both the problem and the solution.

# SMALL GROUP AGREEMENT

## Our Purpose

To transform our spiritual lives by cultivating our spiritual health in a healthy small group community. In addition, we:

_____

_____

_____

## Our Values

| | |
|---|---|
| Group Attendance | To give priority to the group meeting. We will call or e-mail if we will be late or absent. (Completing the _Small Group Calendar_ will minimize this issue.) |
| Safe Environment | To help create a safe place where people can be heard and feel loved. (Please, no quick answers, snap judgments, or simple fixes.) |
| Respect Differences | To be gentle and gracious to people with different spiritual maturity, personal opinions, temperaments, or imperfections. We are all works in progress. |
| Confidentiality | To keep anything that is shared strictly confidential and within the group, and avoid sharing improper information about those outside the group. |
| Encouragement for Growth | To be not just takers but givers of life. We want to spiritually multiply our lives by serving others with our God-given gifts. |

| Welcome for Newcomers | To keep an open chair and share Jesus's dream of finding a shepherd for every sheep. |
| --- | --- |
| Shared Ownership | To remember that every member is a minister and to ensure that each attender will share a small team role or responsibility over time. (See the *Team Roles*.) |
| Rotating Hosts/ Leaders and Homes | To encourage different people to host the group in their homes, and to rotate the responsibility of facilitating each meeting. (See the *Small Group Calendar*.) |

## Our Expectations

- Refreshments/mealtimes _____
- Child care _____
- When we will meet (day of week) _____ - ___
- Where we will meet (place) _____ _____
- We will begin at (time) _____ and end at _____
- We will do our best to have some or all of us attend a worship service together. Our primary worship service time will be _____
- Date of this agreement _____
- Date we will review this agreement again _____
- Who (other than the leader) will review this agreement at the end of this study _____

# TEAM ROLES

The Bible makes clear that every member, not just the small group leader, is a minister in the body of Christ. In a healthy small group, every member takes on some small role or responsibility. It can be more fun and effective if you team up on these roles.

Review the team roles and responsibilities below, and have each member volunteer for a role or participate on a team. If someone doesn't know where to serve or is holding back, as a group, suggest a team or role. It's best to have one or two people on each team so you have each of the five purposes covered. Serving in even a small capacity will not only help your leader but also will make the group more fun for everyone. Don't hold back. Join a team!

The opportunities below are broken down by the five purposes and then by a *crawl* (beginning), *walk* (intermediate), or *run* (advanced) role. Try to cover at least the crawl and walk roles, and select a role that matches your group, your gifts, and your maturity.

| Team Roles | Team Player(s) |
|---|---|
| **CONNECTING TEAM (Fellowship and Community Building)** | |

Crawl: Host a social event or group activity in the first week or two.

Walk: Create a list of uncommitted friends and then invite them to an open house or group social.

Run: Plan a twenty-four-hour retreat or weekend getaway for the group. Lead the *Connecting* time each week for the group.

**GROWING TEAM (Discipleship and Spiritual Growth)**

Crawl: Coordinate the spiritual partners for the group. Facilitate a three- or four-person discussion circle during the Bible study portion of your meeting. Coordinate the discussion circles.

Walk: Tabulate the *Personal Health Plans* in a summary to let people know how you're doing as a group. Encourage personal devotions through group discussions and pairing up with spiritual (accountability) partners.

Run: Take the group on a prayer walk, or plan a day of solitude, fasting, or personal retreat.

**SERVING TEAM (Discovering Your God-Given Design for Ministry)**

Crawl: Ensure that every member finds a group role or team he or she enjoys.

Walk: Have every member take a gift test and determine your group's gifts. Plan a ministry project together.

Run: Help each member decide on a way to use his or her unique gifts somewhere in the church.

**SHARING TEAM (Sharing and Evangelism)**

Crawl: Coordinate the group's *Prayer and Praise Report* of friends and family who don't know Christ.

Walk: Search for group mission opportunities and plan a cross-cultural group activity.

Run: Take a small group "vacation" to host a six-week group in your neighborhood or office. Then come back together with your current group.

**SURRENDERING TEAM (Surrendering Your Heart to Worship)**

Crawl: Maintain the group's *Prayer and Praise Report* or journal.

Walk: Lead a brief time of worship each week (at the beginning or end of your meeting).

Run: Plan a more unique time of worship.

# SMALL GROUP CALENDAR

Planning and calendaring can help ensure the greatest participation at every meeting. At the end of each meeting, review this calendar. Be sure to include a regular rotation of host homes and leaders, and don't forget birthdays, socials, church events, holidays, and mission/ministry projects.

| Date | Lesson | Dessert/Meal | Role |
|------|--------|--------------|------|
|      |        |              |      |
|      |        |              |      |
|      |        |              |      |
|      |        |              |      |
|      |        |              |      |
|      |        |              |      |
|      |        |              |      |
|      |        |              |      |
|      |        |              |      |
|      |        |              |      |
|      |        |              |      |
|      |        |              |      |
|      |        |              |      |
|      |        |              |      |
|      |        |              |      |

# PERSONAL HEALTH ASSESSMENT

| | Just Beginning | Getting Going | Well Developed |
|---|:---:|:---:|:---:|

## CONNECTING with God's Family

| | | |
|---|---|---|
| I am deepening my understanding of and friendship with God in community with others. | | 1 2 3 4 5 |
| I am growing in my ability both to share and to show my love to others. | | 1 2 3 4 5 |
| I am willing to share my real needs for prayer and support from others. | | 1 2 3 4 5 |
| I am resolving conflict constructively and am willing to forgive others. | | 1 2 3 4 5 |
| **CONNECTING** Total | | _____ |

## GROWING to Be Like Christ

| | | |
|---|---|---|
| I have a growing relationship with God through regular time in the Bible and in prayer (spiritual habits). | | 1 2 3 4 5 |
| I am experiencing more of the characteristics of Jesus Christ (love, patience, gentleness, courage, self-control, etc.) in my life. | | 1 2 3 4 5 |
| I am avoiding addictive behaviors (food, television, busyness, and the like) to meet my needs. | | 1 2 3 4 5 |
| I am spending time with a Christian friend (spiritual partner) who celebrates and challenges my spiritual growth. | | 1 2 3 4 5 |
| **GROWING** Total | | _____ |

| | Just Beginning | Getting Going | Well Developed |
|---|---|---|---|

### DEVELOPING Your Gifts to Serve Others

I have discovered and am further developing my unique God-given design.     1 2 3 4 5

I am regularly praying for God to show me opportunities to serve him and others.     1 2 3 4 5

I am serving in a regular (once a month or more) ministry in the church or community.     1 2 3 4 5

I am a team player in my small group by sharing some group role or responsibility.     1 2 3 4 5

**DEVELOPING** Total    _____

### SHARING Your Life Mission Every Day

I am cultivating relationships with non-Christians and praying for God to give me natural opportunities to share his love.     1 2 3 4 5

I am praying and learning about where God can use me and our group cross-culturally for missions.     1 2 3 4 5

I am investing my time in another person or group who needs to know Christ.     1 2 3 4 5

I am regularly inviting unchurched or unconnected friends to my church or small group.     1 2 3 4 5

**SHARING** Total    _____

### SURRENDERING Your Life for God's Pleasure

I am experiencing more of the presence and power of God in my everyday life.     1 2 3 4 5

I am faithfully attending services and my small group to worship God.     1 2 3 4 5

I am seeking to please God by surrendering every area of my life (health, decisions, finances, relationships, future, etc.) to him.     1 2 3 4 5

I am accepting the things I cannot change and becoming increasingly grateful for the life I've been given.     1 2 3 4 5

**SURRENDERING** Total    _____

| | Connecting | Growing | Serving | Sharing | Surrendering | |
|---|---|---|---|---|---|---|
| 20 | | | | | | Well Developed |
| 16 | | | | | | Very Good |
| 12 | | | | | | Getting Going |
| 8 | | | | | | Fair |
| 4 | | | | | | Just Beginning |

○ Beginning Assessment   Total _____
□ Ending Assessment     Total _____

# PERSONAL HEALTH PLAN

This worksheet could become your single most important feature in this study. On it you can record your personal priorities before the Father. It will help you live a healthy spiritual life, balancing all five of God's purposes.

| PURPOSE | PLAN |
|---|---|
| CONNECT | WHO are you connecting with spiritually? |
| GROW | WHAT is your next step for growth? |
| DEVELOP | WHERE are you serving? |
| SHARE | WHEN are you shepherding another in Christ? |
| SURRENDER | HOW are you surrendering your heart to God? |

| DATE | MY PROGRESS | PARTNER'S PROGRESS |
|---|---|---|
| | | |
| | | |
| | | |
| | | |
| | | |

| DATE | MY PROGRESS | PARTNER'S PROGRESS |
|------|-------------|--------------------|
|      |             |                    |
|      |             |                    |
|      |             |                    |
|      |             |                    |
|      |             |                    |
|      |             |                    |
|      |             |                    |
|      |             |                    |
|      |             |                    |
|      |             |                    |
|      |             |                    |
|      |             |                    |
|      |             |                    |
|      |             |                    |
|      |             |                    |
|      |             |                    |
|      |             |                    |
|      |             |                    |
|      |             |                    |
|      |             |                    |
|      |             |                    |

# SAMPLE
# PERSONAL HEALTH PLAN

This worksheet could become your single most important feature in this study. On it you can record your personal priorities before the Father. It will help you live a healthy spiritual life, balancing all five of God's purposes.

| PURPOSE | PLAN |
|---|---|
| CONNECT | WHO are you connecting with spiritually? |
| | Bill and I will meet weekly by e-mail or phone |
| GROW | WHAT is your next step for growth? |
| | Regular devotions or journaling my prayers 2×/week |
| DEVELOP | WHERE are you serving? |
| | Serving in children's ministry<br>Go through GIFTS Assessment |
| SHARE | WHEN are you shepherding another in Christ? |
| | Shepherding Bill at lunch or hosting a starter group in the fall |
| SURRENDER | HOW are you surrendering your heart? |
| | Help with our teenager<br>New job situation |

| DATE | MY PROGRESS | PARTNER'S PROGRESS |
|------|-------------|--------------------|
| 3/5 | Talked during our group | Figured out our goals together |
| 3/12 | Missed our time together | Missed our time together |
| 3/26 | Met for coffee and review of my goals | Met for coffee |
| 4/10 | E-mailed prayer requests | Bill sent me his prayer requests |
| 5/5 | Great start on personal journaling | Read Mark 1–6 in one sitting! |
| 5/12 | Traveled and not doing well this week | Journaled about Christ as healer |
| 5/26 | Back on track | Busy and distracted; asked for prayer |
| 6/1 | Need to call Children's Pastor | |
| 6/26 | Group did a serving project together | Agreed to lead group worship |
| 6/30 | Regularly rotating leadership | Led group worship–great job! |
| | | |
| 7/5 | Called Jim to see if he's open to joining our group | Wanted to invite somebody, but didn't |
| 7/12 | Preparing to start a group in fall | |
| 7/30 | Group prayed for me | Told friend something I'm learning about Christ |
| 8/5 | Overwhelmed but encouraged | Scared to lead worship |
| 8/15 | Felt heard and more settled | Issue with wife |
| 8/30 | Read book on teens | Glad he took on his fear |
| | | |
| | | |
| | | |
| | | |
| | | |
| | | |
| | | |

# SPIRITUAL GIFTS INVENTORY

A spiritual gift is given to each of us as a means of helping the entire church.

1 Corinthians 12:7 (NLT)

A spiritual gift is a special ability, given by the Holy Spirit to every believer at their conversion. Although spiritual gifts are given when the Holy Spirit enters new believers, their use and purpose need to be understood and developed as we grow spiritually. A spiritual gift is much like a muscle; the more you use it, the stronger it becomes.

## A Few Truths about Spiritual Gifts

1. Only believers have spiritual gifts. 1 Corinthians 2:14
2. You can't earn or work for a spiritual gift. Ephesians 4:7
3. The Holy Spirit decides what gifts I get. 1 Corinthians 12:11
4. I am to develop the gifts God gives me. Romans 11:29; 2 Timothy 1:6
5. It's a sin to waste the gifts God gave me. 1 Corinthians 4:1–2; Matthew 25:14–30
6. Using my gifts honors God and expands me. John 15:8

94

## Gifts Inventory

God wants us to know what spiritual gift(s) he has given us. One person can have many gifts. The goal is to find the areas in which the Holy Spirit seems to have supernaturally empowered our service to others. These gifts are to be used to minister to others and build up the body of Christ.

There are four main lists of gifts found in the Bible in Romans 12:3–8; 1 Corinthians 12:1–11, 27–31; Ephesians 4:11–12; and 1 Peter 4:9–11. There are other passages that mention or illustrate gifts not included in these lists. As you read through this list, prayerfully consider whether the biblical definition describes you. Remember, you can have more than one gift, but everyone has at least one.

### ADMINISTRATION (Organization)—1 Corinthians 12

This is the ability to recognize the gifts of others and recruit them to a ministry. It is the ability to organize and manage people, resources, and time for effective ministry.

### APOSTLE—1 Corinthians 12

This is the ability to start new churches/ventures and oversee their development.

### DISCERNMENT—1 Corinthians 12

This is the ability to distinguish between the spirit of truth and the spirit of error; to detect inconsistencies in another's life and confront in love.

### ENCOURAGEMENT (Exhortation)—Romans 12

This is the ability to motivate God's people to apply and act on biblical principles, especially when they are discouraged or wavering in their faith. It is also the ability to bring out the best in others and challenge them to develop their potential.

### EVANGELISM—Ephesians 4

This is the ability to communicate the gospel of Jesus Christ to unbelievers in a positive, nonthreatening way and to sense opportunities to share Christ and lead people to respond with faith.

## FAITH—1 Corinthians 12

This is the ability to trust God for what cannot be seen and to act on God's promise, regardless of what the circumstances indicate. This includes a willingness to risk failure in pursuit of a God-given vision, expecting God to handle the obstacles.

## GIVING—Romans 12

This is the ability to generously contribute material resources and/or money beyond the 10 percent tithe so that the church may grow and be strengthened. It includes the ability to manage money so it may be given to support the ministry of others.

## HOSPITALITY—1 Peter 4:9–10

This is the ability to make others, especially strangers, feel warmly welcomed, accepted, and comfortable in the church family and the ability to coordinate factors that promote fellowship.

## LEADERSHIP—Romans 12

This is the ability to clarify and communicate the purpose and direction ("vision") of a ministry in a way that attracts others to get involved, including the ability to motivate others, by example, to work together in accomplishing a ministry goal.

## MERCY—Romans 12

This is the ability to manifest practical, compassionate, cheerful love toward suffering members of the body of Christ.

## PASTORING (Shepherding)—Ephesians 4

This is the ability to care for the spiritual needs of a group of believers and equip them for ministry. It is also the ability to nurture a small group in spiritual growth and assume responsibility for their welfare.

## PREACHING—Romans 12

This is the ability to publicly communicate God's Word in an inspired way that convinces unbelievers and both challenges and comforts believers.

## SERVICE—Romans 12

This is the ability to recognize unmet needs in the church family, and take the initiative to provide practical assistance quickly, cheerfully, and without a need for recognition.

## TEACHING—Ephesians 4

This is the ability to educate God's people by clearly explaining and applying the Bible in a way that causes them to learn; it is the ability to equip and train other believers for ministry.

## WISDOM—1 Corinthians 12

This is the ability to understand God's perspective on life situations and share those insights in a simple, understandable way.

# TELLING YOUR STORY

First, don't underestimate the power of your testimony. Revelation 12:11 says, "They have defeated [Satan] by the blood of the Lamb and by their testimony. And they did not love their lives so much that they were afraid to die" (NLT).

A simple three-point approach is very effective in communicating your personal testimony. The approach focuses on before you trusted Christ, how you surrendered to him, and the difference in you since you've been walking with him. If you became a Christian at a very young age and don't remember what life was like before Christ, reflect on what you have seen in the lives of others. Before you begin, pray and ask God to give you the right words.

## Before You Knew Christ

Simply tell what your life was like before you surrendered to Christ. What was the key problem, emotion, situation, or attitude you were dealing with? What motivated you? What were your actions? How did you try to satisfy your inner needs? Create an interesting picture of your preconversion life and problems, and then explain what created a need and interest in Christian things.

## How You Came to Know Christ

How were you converted? Simply tell the events and circumstances that caused you to consider Christ as the solution to your needs. Take time to identify the steps that brought you to the point of trusting Christ. Where were you? What was happening at the time? What people or problems influenced your decision?

## The Difference Christ Has Made in Your Life

What is different about your life in Christ? How has his forgiveness impacted you? How have your thoughts, attitudes, and emotions changed? What problems have been resolved or changed? Share how Christ is meeting your needs and what a relationship with him means to you now. This should be the largest part of your story.

## Tips

- Don't use jargon: don't sound churchy, preachy, or pious.
- Stick to the point. Your conversion and new life in Christ should be the main points.
- Be specific. Include events, genuine feelings, and personal insights, both before and after conversion, which people would be interested in and that clarify your main point. This makes your testimony easier to relate to. Assume you are sharing with someone with no knowledge of the Christian faith.
- Be current. Tell what is happening in your life with God now, today.
- Be honest. Don't exaggerate or portray yourself as living a perfect life with no problems. This is not realistic. The simple truth of what God has done in your life is all the Holy Spirit needs to convict someone of their sin and convince them of his love and grace.
- Remember, it's the Holy Spirit who convicts. You need only be obedient and tell your story.
- When people reply to your efforts to share with statements like "I don't believe in God," "I don't believe the Bible is God's Word," or "How can a loving God allow suffering?" how can we respond to these replies?

- Above all, keep a positive attitude. Don't be defensive.
- Be sincere. This will speak volumes about your confidence in your faith.
- Don't be offended. It's not you they are rejecting.
- Pray—silently on-the-spot. Don't proceed without asking for God's help about the specific question. Seek his guidance on how, or if, you should proceed at this time.
- In God's wisdom, choose to do one of the following:
  - Postpone sharing at this time.
  - Answer their objections, if you can.
  - Promise to research their questions and return answers later.

**Step 1.** Everywhere Jesus went he used stories, or parables, to demonstrate our need for salvation. Through these stories, he helped people see the error of their ways, leading them to turn to him. Your story can be just as powerful today. Begin to develop your story by sharing what your life was like before you knew Christ. (If you haven't yet committed your life to Christ, or became a Christian at a very young age and don't remember what life was like before Christ, reflect on what you have seen in the life of someone close to you.) Make notes about this aspect of your story below and commit to writing it out this week.

_____

_____

_____

**Step 2.** Sit in groups of two or three people for this discussion. Review the "How You Came to Know Christ" section. Begin to develop this part of your story by sharing within your circle. Make notes about this aspect of your story below and commit to writing it out this week.

_____

_____

_____

**Step 2b.** Connecting: Go around the group and share about a time you were stopped cold while sharing Christ, by a question you couldn't answer. What happened?

**Step 2c.** Sharing: Previously we talked about the questions and objections we receive that stop us from continuing to share our faith with someone. These questions/objections might include:

- "I don't believe in God."
- "I don't believe the Bible is God's Word."
- "How can a loving God allow suffering?"

How can we respond to these replies?

**Step 3.** Subgroup into groups of two or three people for this discussion. Review "The Difference Christ Has Made in Your Life" section. Share the highlights of this part of your story within your circle. Make notes about this aspect of your story below and commit to writing it out this week.

_____

_____

_____

**Step 3b.** Story: There's nothing more exciting than a brand-new believer. My wife became a Christian four years before I met her. She was a flight attendant at the time. Her zeal to introduce others to Jesus was reminiscent of the woman at the well who ran and got the whole town out to see Jesus.

My wife immediately began an international organization of Christian flight attendants for fellowship and for reaching out to others in their profession. She organized events where many people came to Christ, and bid for trips with another flight attendant who was a Christian so they could witness on the planes. They even bid for the shorter trips so they could talk to as many different people as possible. They had a goal for every flight to talk to at least one person about Christ, and to be encouraged by at least one person who already knew him. God met that request every time.

101

In her zeal, however, she went home to her family over the holidays and vacations and had little or no success. Later she would realize that she pressed them too hard. Jesus said a prophet is without honor in his own town, and I think the same goes for family. That's because members of your family think they know you, and are more likely to ignore changes, choosing instead to see you as they've always seen you. "Isn't this the carpenter's son—the son of Joseph?" they said of Jesus. "Don't we know this guy?"

With family members you have to walk with Christ openly and be patient. Change takes time. And remember, we don't save anyone. We just introduce them to Jesus through telling our own story. God does the rest.

**Step 4.** As a group, review *Telling Your Story*. Share which part of your story is the most difficult for you to tell. Which is the easiest for you? If you have time, a few of you share your story with the group.

**Step 5.** Throughout this study we have had the opportunity to develop our individual testimonies. One way your group can serve each other is to provide a safe forum for "practicing" telling your stories. Continue to take turns sharing your testimonies now. Set a time limit—say two to three minutes each. Don't miss this great opportunity to get to know one another better and encourage each other's growth too.

# SERVING COMMUNION

Churches vary in their treatment of communion (or the Lord's Supper). We offer one simple form by which a small group can share this experience together. You can adapt this as necessary, or omit it from your group altogether, depending on your church's beliefs.

## Steps in Serving Communion

1. Open by sharing about God's love, forgiveness, grace, mercy, commitment, tenderheartedness, faithfulness, etc., out of your personal journey (connect with the stories of those in the room).
2. Read one or several of the passages listed below.
3. Pray and pass the bread around the circle.
4. When everyone has been served, remind them that this represents Jesus's broken body on their behalf. Simply state, "Jesus said, 'Do this in remembrance of me' (Luke 22:19 NIV). Let us eat together," and eat the bread as a group.
5. Then read the rest of the passage: "In the same way, after the supper he took the cup, saying, 'This cup is the new covenant in my blood, which is poured out for you'" (Luke 22:20 NIV).
6. Pray, and serve the cups, either by passing a small tray, serving them individually, or having members pick up a cup from the table.
7. When everyone has been served, remind them the juice represents Christ's blood shed for them, then simply state, "Take and drink in remembrance of him. Let us drink together."
8. Finish by singing a simple song, listening to a praise song, or having a time of prayer in thanks to God.

Communion passages: Matthew 26:26–29; Mark 14:22–25; Luke 22:14–20; 1 Corinthians 10:16–21; 11:17–34.

# PERFORMING A FOOTWASHING

*Scripture:* John 13:1–17. Jesus makes it quite clear to his disciples that his position as the Father's Son includes being a servant rather than power and glory only. To properly understand the scene and the intention of Jesus, we must realize that the washing of feet was the duty of slaves and indeed of non-Jewish rather than Jewish slaves. Jesus placed himself in the position of a servant. He displayed to the disciples self-sacrifice and love. In view of his majesty, only the symbolic position of a slave was adequate to open their eyes and keep them from lofty illusions. The point of footwashing, then, is to correct the attitude that Jesus discerned in the disciples. It constitutes the permanent basis for mutual service, service in your group and for the community around you, which is the responsibility of all Christians.

## When to Implement

There are three primary places we would recommend you insert a footwashing: during a break in the Surrendering section of your group; during a break in the Growing section of your group; or at the closing of your group. A special time of prayer for each person as he or she gets his or her feet washed can be added to the foot-washing time.

# SURRENDERING AT THE CROSS

Surrendering everything to God is one of the most challenging aspects of following Jesus. It involves a relationship built on trust and faith. Each of us is in a different place on our spiritual journey. Some of us have known the Lord for many years, some are new in our faith, and some may still be checking God out. Regardless, we all have things that we still want control over—things we don't want to give to God because we don't know what he will do with them. These things are truly more important to us than God is—they have become our god.

We need to understand that God wants us to be completely devoted to him. If we truly love God with all our heart, soul, strength, and mind (Luke 10:27), we will be willing to give him everything.

## Steps in Surrendering at the Cross

1. You will need some small pieces of paper and pens or pencils for people to write down the things they want to sacrifice/surrender to God.
2. If you have a wooden cross, hammers, and nails you can have the members nail their sacrifices to the cross. If you don't have a wooden cross, get creative. Think of another way to symbolically relinquish the sacrifices to God. You might use a fireplace to burn them in the fire as an offering to the Lord. The point is giving to the Lord whatever hinders your relationship with him.

3. Create an atmosphere conducive to quiet reflection and prayer. Whatever this quiet atmosphere looks like for your group, do the best you can to create a peaceful time to meet with God.

4. Once you are settled, prayerfully think about the points below. Let the words and thoughts draw you into a heart-to-heart connection with your Lord Jesus Christ.

   ☐ *Worship him.* Ask God to change your viewpoint so you can worship him through a surrendered spirit.

   ☐ *Humble yourself.* Surrender doesn't happen without humility. James 4:6–7 says: "'God opposes the proud but gives grace to the humble.' Submit yourselves, then, to God" (NIV).

   ☐ *Surrender your mind, will, and emotions.* This is often the toughest part of surrendering. What do you sense God urging you to give him so you can have the kind of intimacy he desires with you? Our hearts yearn for this kind of connection with him; let go of the things that stand between you.

   ☐ *Write out your prayer.* Write out your prayer of sacrifice and surrender to the Lord. This may be an attitude, a fear, a person, a job, a possession—anything that God reveals is a hindrance to your relationship with him.

5. After writing out your sacrifice, take it to the cross and offer it to the Lord. Nail your sacrifice to the cross, or burn it as a sacrifice in the fire.

6. Close by singing, praying together, or taking communion. Make this time as short or as long as seems appropriate for your group.

Surrendering to God is life-changing and liberating. God desires that we be overcomers! First John 4:4 says, "You, dear children, are from God and have overcome . . . because the one who is in you is greater than the one who is in the world" (NIV).

# JOURNALING 101

Henri Nouwen says effective and lasting ministry *for* God grows out of a quiet place alone *with* God. This is why journaling is so important.

The greatest adventure of our lives is found in the daily pursuit of knowing, growing in, serving, sharing, and worshiping Christ forever. This is the essence of a purposeful life: to see all these biblical purposes fully formed and balanced in our lives. Only then are we "complete in Christ" (Col. 1:28 NASB).

David poured his heart out to God by writing psalms. The book of Psalms contains many of his honest conversations with God in written form, including expressions of every imaginable emotion on every aspect of his life. Like David, we encourage you to select a strategy to integrate God's Word and journaling into your devotional time. Use any of the following resources:

- Bible
- Bible reading plan
- Devotional
- Topical Bible study plan

Before and after you read a portion of God's Word, speak to God in honest reflection in the form of a written prayer. You may begin this time by simply finishing the sentence "Father, . . . ," "Yesterday, Lord, . . . ," or "Thank you, God, for, . . . ." Share with him where you are at the present moment; express your hurts, disappointments, frustrations, blessings, victories, and gratefulness. Whatever you do with your journal, make a plan that fits you, so you'll have a positive experience. Consider sharing highlights of your progress and experiences with some or all of your group members, especially your spiritual partner. You may find they want to join and even encourage you in this journey. Most of all, enjoy the ride and cultivate a more authentic, growing walk with God.

# PRAYER AND PRAISE REPORT

Briefly share your prayer requests with the large group, making notations below. Then gather in small groups of two to four to pray for each other.

Date: _____

Prayer Requests

_____

_____

_____

_____

_____

Praise Reports

_____

_____

_____

_____

_____

## Prayer and Praise Report

Briefly share your prayer requests with the large group, making notations below. Then gather in small groups of two to four to pray for each other.

Date: _____

Prayer Requests

_____

_____

_____

_____

_____

Praise Reports

_____

_____

_____

_____

_____

## Prayer and Praise Report

Briefly share your prayer requests with the large group, making notations below. Then gather in small groups of two to four to pray for each other.

Date: _____

Prayer Requests

_____

_____

_____

_____

_____

## Praise Reports

_____

_____

_____

_____

_____

## Prayer and Praise Report

Briefly share your prayer requests with the large group, making notations below. Then gather in small groups of two to four to pray for each other.

Date: _____

## Prayer Requests

_____

_____

_____

_____

_____

## Praise Reports

_____

_____

_____

_____

_____

111

## Prayer and Praise Report

Briefly share your prayer requests with the large group, making notations below. Then gather in small groups of two to four to pray for each other.

Date: _____

Prayer Requests

_____

_____

_____

_____

_____

Praise Reports

_____

_____

_____

_____

_____

# SMALL GROUP ROSTER

| Name | Address | Phone | E-mail Address | Team or Role | When/How to Contact You |
|------|---------|-------|----------------|--------------|-------------------------|
| Bill Jones | 7 Alvalar Street L.F. 92665 | 766-2255 | bjones@aol.com | Socials | Evenings After 5 |
|  |  |  |  |  |  |
|  |  |  |  |  |  |
|  |  |  |  |  |  |
|  |  |  |  |  |  |
|  |  |  |  |  |  |
|  |  |  |  |  |  |
|  |  |  |  |  |  |
|  |  |  |  |  |  |

(Pass your book around your group at your first meeting to get everyone's name and contact information.)

| Name | Address | Phone | E-mail Address | Team or Role | When/How to Contact You |
|------|---------|-------|----------------|--------------|-------------------------|
|      |         |       |                |              |                         |
|      |         |       |                |              |                         |
|      |         |       |                |              |                         |
|      |         |       |                |              |                         |
|      |         |       |                |              |                         |
|      |         |       |                |              |                         |
|      |         |       |                |              |                         |
|      |         |       |                |              |                         |
|      |         |       |                |              |                         |

# LEADING FOR THE FIRST TIME
## LEADERSHIP 101

**Sweaty palms are a healthy sign.** The Bible says God is gracious to the humble. Remember who is in control; the time to worry is when you're not worried. Those who are soft in heart (and sweaty-palmed) are those whom God is sure to speak through.

**Seek support.** Ask your leader, coleader, or close friend to pray for you and prepare with you before the session. Walking through the study will help you anticipate potentially difficult questions and discussion topics.

**Bring your uniqueness to the study.** Lean into who you are and how God wants you to uniquely lead the study.

**Prepare. Prepare. Prepare.** Go through the session several times. If you are using the DVD, listen to the teaching segment and *Leader Lifter*. Consider writing in a journal or fasting for a day to prepare yourself for what God wants to do.

**Don't wait until the last minute to prepare.**

**Ask for feedback so you can grow.** Perhaps in an e-mail or on cards handed out at the study, have everyone write down three things you did well and one thing you could improve on. Don't get defensive, but show an openness to learn and grow.

**Prayerfully consider launching a new group.** This doesn't need to happen overnight, but God's heart is for this to happen over time. Not all Christians are called to be leaders or teachers, but we are all called to be "shepherds" of a few someday.

**Share with your group what God is doing in your heart.** God is searching for those whose hearts are fully his. Share your trials and victories. We promise that people will relate.

**Prayerfully consider whom you would like to pass the baton to next week.** It's only fair. God is ready for the next member of your group to go on the faith journey you just traveled. Make it fun, and expect God to do the rest.

# LEADER'S NOTES
## INTRODUCTION

Congratulations! You have responded to the call to help shepherd Jesus's flock. There are few other tasks in the family of God that surpass the contribution you will be making. We have provided you several ways to prepare for this role. Between the *Read Me First*, these *Leader's Notes*, and the *Watch This First* and *Leader Lifter* segments on the optional *Deepening Life Together: Romans* Video Teaching DVD, you'll have all you need to do a great job of leading your group. Just don't forget, you are not alone. God knew that you would be asked to lead this group and he won't let you down. In Hebrews 13:5b God promises us, "Never will I leave you; never will I forsake you" (NIV).

Your role as leader is to create a safe, warm environment for your group. As a leader, your most important job is to create an atmosphere where people are willing to talk honestly about what the topics discussed in this study have to do with them. Be available before people arrive so you can greet them at the door. People are naturally nervous at a new group, so a hug or handshake can help put them at ease. Before you start leading your group, a little preparation will give you confidence. Review the *Read Me First* at the front of your study guide so you'll understand the purpose of each section, enabling you to help your group understand it as well.

117

If you're new to leading a group, congratulations and thank you; this will be a life-changing experience for you also. We have provided these *Leader's Notes* to help new leaders begin well.

It's important in your first meeting to make sure group members understand that things shared personally and in prayer must remain confidential. Also, be careful not to dominate the group discussion, but facilitate it and encourage others to join in and share. And lastly, have fun.

Take a moment at the beginning of your first meeting to orient the group to one principle that undergirds this study: A healthy small group balances the purposes of the church. Most small groups emphasize Bible study, fellowship, and prayer. But God has called us to reach out to others as well. He wants us to do what Jesus teaches, not just learn about it.

**Preparing for each meeting ahead of time.** Take the time to review the session, the *Leader's Notes*, and *Leader Lifter* for the session before each session. Also write down your answers to each question. Pay special attention to exercises that ask group members to *do* something. These exercises will help your group live out what the Bible teaches, not just talk about it. Be sure you understand how the exercises work, and bring any supplies you might need, such as paper or pens. Pray for your group members by name at least once between sessions and before each session. Use the *Prayer and Praise Report* so you will remember their prayer requests. Ask God to use your time together to touch the heart of every person. Expect God to give you the opportunity to talk with those he wants you to encourage or challenge in a special way.

**Don't try to go it alone.** Pray for God to help you. Ask other members of your group to help by taking on some small role. In the *Appendix* you'll find the *Team Roles* pages with some suggestions to get people involved. Leading is more rewarding if you give group members opportunities to help. Besides, helping group members discover their individual gifts for serving or even leading the group will bless all of you.

Consider asking a few people to come early to help set up, pray, and introduce newcomers to others. Even if everyone is new, they don't know that yet and may be shy when they arrive. You might give people roles like setting up name tags or handing out drinks. This could be a great way to spot a co-leader.

**Subgrouping.** If your group has more than seven people, break into discussion groups of three to four people for the *Growing* and *Surrendering* sections each week. People will connect more with the study and each other when they have more opportunity to participate. Smaller discussion circles encourage quieter people to talk more and tend to minimize the effects of more vocal or dominant members. Also, people who are unaccustomed to praying aloud will feel more comfortable praying within a smaller group of people. Share prayer requests in the larger group and then break into smaller groups to pray for each other. People are more willing to pray in small circles if they know that the whole group will hear all the prayer requests.

**Memorizing Scripture.** At the start of each session you will find a memory verse—a verse for the group to memorize each week. Encourage your group members to do this. Memorizing God's Word is both directed and celebrated throughout the Bible, either explicitly ("Your word I have hidden in my heart, that I might not sin against You" [Ps. 119:11 NKJV]), or implicitly, as in the example of our Lord ("He departed to the mountain to pray" [Mark 6:46 NKJV]).

Anyone who has memorized Scripture can confirm the amazing spiritual benefits that result from this practice. Don't miss out on the opportunity to encourage your group to grow in the knowledge of God's Word through Scripture memorization.

**Reflections.** We've provided opportunity for a personal time with God using the *Reflections* at the end of each session. Don't press seekers to do this, but just remind the group that every believer should have a plan for personal time with God.

**Inviting new people.** Cast the vision, as Jesus did, to be inclusive not exclusive. Ask everyone to prayerfully think of people who would enjoy or benefit from a group like this—then invite them. The beginning of a new study is a great time to welcome a few people into your circle. Don't worry about ending up with too many people—you can always have one discussion circle in the living room and another in the dining room.

**For Deeper Study (Optional).** We have included a *For Deeper Study* section in each session. *For Deeper Study* provides additional passages for individual study on the topic of each session. If your group likes to do deeper Bible study, consider having members study the *For Deeper Study* passages for homework. Then, during the *Growing* portion of your meeting, you can share the high points of what you've learned.

# LEADER'S NOTES
## SESSIONS

### Session One  An Introduction to Romans

*Connecting*

1. We've designed this study for both new and established groups, and for both seekers and the spiritually mature. New groups will need to invest more time building relationships with each other. Established groups often want to dig deeper into Bible study and application. Regardless of whether your group is new or has been together for a while, be sure to answer this introductory question at this first session.

2. A very important item in this first session is the *Small Group Agreement*. An agreement helps clarify your group's priorities and cast new vision for what the group can become. You can find this in the *Appendix* of this study guide. We've found that groups that talk about these values up front and commit to an agreement benefit significantly. They work through conflicts long before people get to the point of frustration, so there's a lot less pain.

   Take some time to review this agreement before your meeting. Then during your meeting, read the agreement aloud to the entire group. If some people have concerns about a specific item or the agreement as a whole, be sensitive to their concerns. Explain that tens of thousands of groups use agreements like this one as a simple tool for building trust and group health over time.

   We recommend talking about shared ownership of the group. It's important that each member have a role. See the *Appendix* to learn more about *Team Roles*. This is a great tool to get this important practice launched in your group.

   If your group is new, you may want to focus on welcoming newcomers or on sharing group ownership. Any group will quickly move from being

121

"the leader's group" to "our group" if everyone understands the goals of the group and shares a small role. See the *Team Roles* in the *Appendix* for help on how to do this well.

## Growing

Have someone read Bible passages aloud. It's a good idea to ask ahead of time, because not everyone is comfortable reading aloud in public.

4. The gospel is God's. The Old Testament prophets pointed toward it. It is about God's Son, who is fully human in that he descended from King David, but who is also divine. His bodily resurrection from the dead is proof of this, and this resurrection lies at the core of the good news. Also central is that the good news calls people to have faith in Christ, and this faith involves obeying him. It is trust revealed in action. The good news also involves God using his power to save those who have this kind of faith in him. Save them from what? Romans will explain that. Righteousness, too, is central to this news.

    Write these questions down, and look at them again at the end of this study to see which have been answered. This study will be too brief to answer all of your questions, but it should answer many. Maybe someone in the group would like the job of tracking down answers to any questions that remain unanswered by the end of the study.

5. Faith isn't just an intellectual agreement with a list of information about Jesus Christ. It is trust in him as a person. Trusting him involves doing what he says to do. The first eight chapters of Romans detail what God has done for us through Christ. Chapters 12–15 describe how we respond in faithful obedience. The Holy Spirit plays an essential role in enabling us to live (obey) by faith.

6. "Righteousness" and "justification" translate the same Greek word. Righteousness is about justice. Most of us want to be treated justly, and we're genuinely upset when we see terrible injustices committed against us or other people. But many people today find it hard to see their faults as serious enough to warrant the kind of wrath (1:18) that Paul talks about in Romans. They think Christians should emphasize God's love and stop talking about wrath, hell, and so on. In session 2 we'll look at Paul's argument for why we should see ourselves as wrongdoers. He's not interested in fostering neurotic guilt over insignificant matters. Rather, he wants us to come to grips with the ways we genuinely insult God and harm others.

7. Salvation is first for Jews, then for Gentiles. That may seem like God is playing favorites. But God also judges the wrongdoing of Jews first, then Gentiles. God doesn't play favorites, but he has a plan for each group. In

Romans 9–11 Paul has a lot to say about the role Jews and Gentiles each play in God's plan.

8. It is important to understand the universality of sin and rebellion because all are accountable to God. No one is made right with God unless they are willing to face their own sinfulness.

11. We have been called according to his purpose to be conformed to the image of his Son, to be made like him in character. God justified us, bringing us into a restored, intimate relationship with himself. With the Holy Spirit's help, we increasingly become people who do what is just and right. Glory is our destiny. The Spirit intercedes for us with God, so that nothing can separate us from his love.

12. Living a life that is acceptable to God is an act of worship. It's not about us; it is about God—giving all that we are and have to him. We offer our bodies completely; we allow our minds to be transformed. We are able to do this by trusting Christ and responding to the guidance and power of the Holy Spirit.

## Developing

This section enables you to help the group see the importance of developing their abilities for service to God.

14. The intent of this question is to encourage group members to set aside some time to spend with God in prayer and his Word at home each day throughout the week. Read through this section and be prepared to help the group understand how important it is to fill our minds with the Word of God. If people already have a commitment to a good Bible reading plan, that is great, but you may have people who struggle to stay in the Word daily. Sometimes beginning with a simple commitment to a short daily reading can start a habit that changes their life.

The *Reflections* pages at the end of each session include verses that were either talked about in the session or support the teaching of the session. They are very short readings with a few lines to encourage people to write down their thoughts. Remind the group about these *Reflections* each week during the *Surrendering* section. Encourage the group to see the importance of making this time to connect with God a priority in their life. Offer further encouragement to commit to a next step in prayer, Bible reading, or meditation on the Word.

Suggested exercise: To help the group get started with meditating on the Word of God, provide everyone with a 3×5 index card. Have everyone write this week's memory verse on the card and begin memorizing Scripture together.

## Sharing

Jesus wants all of his disciples to help outsiders connect with him, to know him personally. This section should provide an opportunity to go beyond Bible study to biblical living.

## Surrendering

God is most pleased by a heart that is fully his. Each group session will provide group members a chance to surrender their hearts to God in prayer and worship. Group prayer requests and prayer time should be included every week.

15. Singing a song of praise, reading Scripture aloud together, or speaking words of praise to God are all excellent ways of focusing our attention on God for a time of surrender. Each session includes an activity that will help the group achieve an attitude of praise and worship.

16. Encourage group members to use the *Reflections* verses in their daily quiet time throughout the week. This will move them closer to God while reinforcing the lesson of this session through related Scripture.

17. As you move to a time of sharing prayer requests, be sure to remind the group of the importance of confidentiality and keeping what is shared in the group within the group. Everyone must feel that the personal things they share will be kept in confidence if you are to have safety and bonding among the group members.

    Use the *Prayer and Praise Report* in the *Appendix* to record your prayer requests. There you can keep track of requests and celebrate answers to prayer.

## For Deeper Study

We have included an optional *For Deeper Study* section in each session. *For Deeper Study* provides additional passages for individual study on the topic of each session. If your group likes to do deeper Bible study, consider having members study the *For Deeper Study* passages at home between meetings.

## Session Two  Condemnation

*Connecting*

2. Encourage group members to take time to complete the *Personal Health Assessment* and pair up with someone to discuss one thing that is going well and one thing that needs work. Participants should not be asked to share any aspect of this assessment in the large group if they don't want to. We will refer back to this exercise in future sessions.

3. We encourage the group to rotate leaders and host homes each meeting. This practice will go a long way toward bonding the group. Review the *Small Group Calendar* and talk about who else is willing to open their home or facilitate a meeting. Rotating host homes and leadership along with implementing *Team Roles* as discussed in *Session One*, will quickly move the group ownership from "your group" to "our group."

*Growing*

This session covers significant portions of Romans chapters 1 through 3. Reading the entire selection aloud may be time-consuming so we recommend that you ask the group to read these passages at home before coming to the group.

5. Encourage the group to talk about the things they see around them that prove God's existence and power. A few examples are: the earth and galaxy that contains it, the presence of so many species of living things that feed and otherwise sustain each other, the nature and nurture of humankind for each other and the environment, and the ability of people to discern what is right and wrong. Because of all this, we "are without excuse" when we choose to turn from God's ways to the ways of the world.

7. Brainstorm some ideas here on how people judge others, but don't allow the group to dwell too much on any specific example of judgment. The point of this discussion is to bring out the judgmental nature of our hearts; so an example might be something simple and seemingly inconsequencial like the snap judgments we tend to make toward others because of how they look, the pitch of their voice, the car they drive, etc.

8. God is a just God. He will not judge us on the basis of our circumstances, whether we grew up in a Christian family and took our children to church, or how much money we made. God will judge us based on who we are at our core and what we have done for his name. On the Day of Judgment we will receive what is due us according to our persistence in obedience to God's will. We will see later in Romans that salvation is a free gift of grace to those who put their faith in Christ. It is not earned. But as we see in this

passage, "works," or actions, still matter. Actions reflect what we really believe and who we really trust. We can never do enough good actions to earn salvation without trusting in the death of Christ for our sins, but we are still accountable to God for what our actions say about our hearts.

9. The Jews' huge advantage was that they had the words of God, the Hebrew Bible, which we now call the Old Testament. They had the laws God gave Moses to shape a godly society, they had the sacrificial system that showed the seriousness of sin and gave a way for it to be dealt with, they had the history of Israel's wrongdoing as a model to avoid, and they had the teachings of the prophets about right and wrong living. They had so much more insight into God's heart than the pagans did. But just having the Bible wasn't enough. Just reading and even meditating on the Bible wasn't enough to make them a holy people. Some ignored the Bible's teachings, and others made a complex system of obeying the law that frequently missed the point of what God was after. The Hebrew Bible was and is incredibly good, but it was powerless to transform the human heart. That was never its purpose.

10. The point of these passages is to help us understand that no one since Adam and Eve has been righteous before God at birth. We become righteous as we become consicous of sin and surrender it and our lives to God.

## Developing

12. For many, spiritual partners will be a new idea. We highly encourage you to try pairs for this study. It's so hard to start a spiritual practice like prayer or consistent Bible reading with no support. A friend makes a huge difference. As leader, you may want to prayerfully decide who would be a good match with whom. Remind people that this partnership isn't forever; it's just for a few weeks. Be sure to have extra copies of the *Personal Health Plan* available at this meeting in case you need to have a group of three spiritual partners. It is a good idea for you to look over the *Personal Health Plan* before the meeting so you can help people understand how to use it.

Instruct your group members to enlist a spiritual partner by asking them to pair up with someone in the group (we suggest that men partner with men and women with women) and turn to the *Personal Health Plan* in the *Appendix*.

Ask the group to complete the instructions in the session for the WHO and WHAT questions on the *Personal Health Plan*. Your group has now begun to address two of God's purposes for their lives!

You can see that the *Personal Health Plan* contains space to record the ups and downs and progress each week in the column labeled "My Progress." When partners check in each week, they can record their partner's progress in the goal he or she chose in the "Partner's Progress" column on this chart. In the *Appendix* you'll find a *Sample Personal Health Plan* filled in as an example.

The WHERE, WHEN, and HOW questions on the *Personal Health Plan* will be addressed in future sessions of the study.

15. A *Circles of Life* diagram is provided for you and the group to use to help you identify people who need a connection to Christian community. Encourage the group to commit to praying for God's guidance and an opportunity to reach out to each person in their *Circles of Life*.

We encourage this outward focus for your group because groups that become too inwardly focused tend to become unhealthy over time. People naturally gravitate toward feeding themselves through Bible study, prayer, and social time, so it's usually up to the leader to push them to consider how this inward nourishment can overflow into outward concern for others. Never forget: Jesus came to seek and save the lost and to find a shepherd for every sheep.

Talk to the group about the importance of inviting people; remind them that healthy small groups make a habit of inviting friends, neighbors, unconnected church members, co-workers, etc., to join their groups or join them at a weekend service. When people get connected to a group of new friends, they often join the church.

Some groups are happy with the people they already have in the group and they don't really want to grow larger. Some fear that newcomers will interrupt the intimacy that members have built over time. However, groups generally gain strength with the infusion of new people. It's like a river of living water flowing into a stagnant pond. Some groups remain permanently open, while others open periodically, such as at the beginning and ending of a study. If your circle becomes too large for easy face-to-face conversations, you can simply form a second or third discussion circle in another room in your home.

*Surrendering*

If your group is large, don't forget to break into groups of three to four people for the prayer time in the *Surrendering* section of your study to ensure that everyone receives prayer. Remember to share prayer requests in the larger group before breaking into smaller groups to pray for each other.

17. Last week we talked briefly about incorporating *Reflections* into the group members' daily time with God. Some people don't yet have an established quiet time. With this in mind, engage in a discussion with the group about the importance of making daily time with God a priority. Talk about potential obstacles and practical ideas for overcoming them. The *Reflections* verses could serve as a springboard for drawing near to God. So don't forget these are a valuable resource for your group.

18. Be sure to remind the group of the importance of confidentiality and keeping what is shared in the group within the group. Use the *Prayer and Praise Report* in the *Appendix* to record your prayer requests.

## Session Three  Justification

*Growing*

This session covers significant portions of Romans chapter 3 and all of chapters 4 through 5. Reading the entire selection aloud may be time-consuming so we recommend that you ask the group to read these passages at home before coming to the group.

3. The final goal of God's plan is justification for all who are willing to respond in faith, both Jews and Gentiles. Although the Lord Jesus has paid the price for our justification, it is through our faith that we receive him and are clothed in his righteousness.

4. Those who have been churchgoers for a while may take the idea of Jesus's death for granted. But while animal sacrifice was common in Paul's day, it doesn't exist in our society, so you may need to take the time to talk through why God would have to have anybody die—not just pay a price, but actually die—because of the wrongs of the members of your group, who are probably fine people.

5. The pathway to righteousness is faith in Jesus Christ. We will see later that faith includes a response of action, but the actions don't earn God's favor. The shed blood of Christ is our confidence; actions are a response of gratitude, or else they are meaningless.

7. Abraham received the sign of circumcision, a seal of the righteousness that he already had by faith while he was still uncircumcised. So then, he is the father of all who believe but have not been circumcised, and also of those who believe and are circumcised. Abraham is the father of all those who respond to God's grace with faith. Circumcision was secondary to faith.

10. God gives them peace with him, access to him, hope, perseverance, character, and love. And suffering. We'd like to skip over that, but suffering is inevitable for humans whether we believe in Christ or not. The difference Christ makes when we suffer is that the Holy Spirit provides resources to enable us to develop character from suffering, rather than just becoming bitter and despairing.

*Developing*

11. Group members who are currently serving the body of Christ in some capacity should be encouraged to share their experiences with the group as a way to encourage them. All group members should consider where they could take a next step toward getting involved in ministry. Discuss some of the ministries that your church may offer to people looking to get involved, such as the children's ministry, ushering, or hospitality. Remind everyone that it sometimes takes time and trying several different ministries before finding the one that fits best.

12. Encourage group members to use the *Personal Health Plan* to jot down their next step to serving in ministry, with a plan for how and when they will begin.

*Sharing*

14. It is important to return to the *Circles of Life* and encourage the group to follow through in their commitments to invite people who need to know Christ more deeply through Christian community. When people are asked why they never go to church they often say, "No one ever invited me." Remind the group that our responsibility is to invite people, but it is the Holy Spirit's responsibility to compel them to come.

## Session Four  Sanctification

*Growing*

This session covers all of chapters 6 through 8. Consider asking the group to read these passages at home before coming to the group.

3. When we put our faith in Christ, who died and was raised to new life, we die to sin in order to live a new life—one in which we are able to resist the temptation to sin with Christ's help. We have died to sin. We are no longer slaves to sin.

4. This is huge. Christians need to know the freedom Christ gives them to choose against sin. Paul's opponents charged that if people knew they'd be forgiven no matter what, they would sin unrestrainedly. But Paul says no real Christian wants to live mired in sin. Real Christians have died to sin's enslavement and are thrilled to be free to live godly lives. No sane person wants to be free to sin; sane people who understand sin want to be free not to sin.

   Addiction and other compulsive habits give a good picture of what it's like to be enslaved to sin. A person can hate a habit and still be powerless to stop it. Dying to sin through Christ makes it possible for us to start breaking those destructive habits.

5. We don't do this by sheer willpower. Paul will talk in chapter 8 about how the Holy Spirit helps us. But we do have to choose constantly to remind ourselves that we're dead to sin, that no sane person wants to sin. We need to take the trouble to look very hard at a tempting sin and push ourselves to see how much harm it will do. We need to consciously offer ourselves to God. Spiritual practices like prayer, reflection on the Scriptures, and honesty with fellow believers are invaluable.

6. We are slaves of one or the other. Christians commit sins, and many of us fight long battles with besetting sins. But to say, "My enslavement to this bad temper is okay" isn't an option for Paul, because fundamentally one is a slave either to sin or to God. We can't have it both ways. "The benefit you reap leads to holiness, and the result is eternal life" (Rom. 6:22b NIV).

8. The end result of life in the flesh is eternal spiritual death. The end result of life in the Spirit is eternal spiritual life with God. Life in the Spirit involves freedom from condemnation, freedom from the compulsion to sin, life and peace by setting one's mind on what the Spirit desires.

9. Transformation is a partnership between us and the Spirit. We take the trouble to learn to listen to him through prayer and the Scriptures. We struggle against sin and cry out for his help. We seek his help through the support of fellow Christians. The Spirit prays for us. He is committed to working in us for our good, to conform us to the likeness of Christ.

10. Our future hope is glory, the redemption of our bodies and the renewal of all creation.

11. Romans 8:28 gives us assurance that God, the sovereign creator of the universe, is for us. Nothing can separate us from his love. Becoming like Christ isn't easy, and sometimes we get frustrated with life or with ourselves. At those times, we need to bask in the awareness of how deeply we are loved.

## Developing

12. Point the group to the *Spiritual Gifts Inventory* in the *Appendix*. Read through the spiritual gifts and engage the group in discussion about which gifts they believe they have. Encourage them to review these further on their own time during the coming week, giving prayerful consideration to each one. We will refer back to this again later in the study.

*Sharing*

This activity provides an opportunity for the group to share Jesus in a very practical way. Discuss this with everyone and choose one action step to take as a group. Be certain that everyone understands his or her role in this activity. It might be a good idea to call each person during the week to be sure they don't forget to bring to the next session what is required of them.

Designate one person to investigate where to donate items in your area. That person can also be responsible for dropping off the items.

Encourage group members to think about when they are shepherding another person in Christ. This could be simply following through on inviting someone to church or reaching out to them in Christ's love. Then have everyone answer the question "WHEN are you shepherding another person in Christ?" on the *Personal Health Plan*.

**Session Five  God's Plan for His Chosen People Israel**

*Growing*

This session covers all of chapters 9 through 11. Consider asking the group to read these passages at home before coming to the group.

3. While the major theme of chapters 9–11 is God's dealing with his chosen people, the underlying theme is God's sovereignty in doing so—his complete authority to choose whom and what he wants. Paul declares that Israel's unbelief is consistent with God's sovereign purpose; all of their unique God-given advantages were useless if they rejected his Son as Savior and Lord (vv. 4–5). The word sovereignty is not found in Scripture, but the concept—that God is free to act as he chooses, without any limits set by the actions of another—is deeply rooted in the biblical concept of God.

4. The issue is not justice but sovereign decision. As the sovereign God, he has the right to choose to show mercy to whomever he wants. In fact, he is not under obligation to extend mercy to anyone. Therefore, experiencing God's mercy doesn't depend on what we want or on our effort. No one deserves mercy—by definition, mercy is undeserved kindness. Esau didn't get less than he deserved; Jacob got more than he deserved.

5. God has mercy on whom he wants to have mercy and he hardens (makes stubborn) whom he wants to harden. This shows that God chooses and works sovereignly, but not arbitrarily. Ultimately, Pharaoh was responsible for his own actions when he was cruel to the enslaved Israelites. The book of Exodus says both that Pharaoh hardened his own heart and that God hardened Pharaoh's heart. Pharaoh's choices worked within God's sovereign

will, but Pharaoh wasn't a helpless robot. (You can find the story of Pharaoh in Exodus 3–14.) The issue is whether God is allowed to create bad people who will reject him and do bad things. It can be hard to accept that this is God's universe, he made it, and he gets to run it. He is wiser and stronger than we are, and he is also more good and loving than we can grasp. Do we have the right to criticize God for creating Hitler? Paul says no. But it's an important question to grapple with, because many people harbor feelings that God isn't really good, and this is one reason they cite.

6. Paul says Israel's failure to respond to the proclamation of the Gospel is not because they don't have the information. It is because they are rebellious and unbelieving. At the same time, God has not withheld salvation from them. He holds out his hands, imploring them to return to him. And some do. Paul is pretty hard on his fellow Jews, but given the history of Christian-Jewish relations, we need to be careful to be patient and respectful. A crucified Messiah really is hard to swallow. Most of the New Testament writers, including Paul, spend a lot of time explaining how that could possibly make sense. Before we judge our Jewish neighbors harshly, we should look at the matter from their perspective.

9. "Because of their transgression, salvation has come to the Gentiles to make Israel envious" (Rom. 11:11 NIV). Israel's rejection of God's plan served at least two divine purposes: 1) Ironically, it helps to bring salvation to the Gentiles, and 2) It makes Israel jealous, which Paul hopes will eventually lead them back to their Messiah.

10. Gentile Christians have been grafted into a tree whose root is thoroughly Jewish. Jesus is Jewish. Paul is Jewish. The Bible is steeped in a Jewish outlook. Gentile Christians should be grateful to Jews for those roots and constantly mindful that it is a privilege to be grafted in. If Gentiles who call themselves Christians live by unbelief, they will be torn away from the trunk in the same way that unbelieving Jews were torn away. Gentiles are in no way ethnically superior to Jews—the only thing that counts is living by belief or unbelief in Christ.

## Developing

12. If members of the group have committed to spending time alone with God, congratulate them and encourage them to take their commitment one step further and begin journaling. Review *Journaling 101* in the *Appendix* prior to your group meeting so that you are familiar with what it contains.

13. It's time to start thinking about what your group will do when you're finished with this study. Now is the time to ask how many people will be joining you so you can choose a study and have the books available when you meet for the next session.

*Sharing*

14. Discuss the implication of Jesus's mandate to take the Gospel to the "ends of the earth" on the lives of believers today. Have each person consider the action steps listed in this question and choose one to begin immediately as a way of doing their part in seeing this accomplished.

## Session Six  Living Out This New Life, Part 1

*Growing*

6. An inflated view of oneself is out of place in the Christian life. Rather, we should use the sound thinking abilities that God gives us to develop a proper sense of humility and an awareness of the need to be involved with other members of Christ's body.

7. Some of the roles and responsibilities of people in the church are: prophecy, serving (particularly those in need), teaching, exhortation, generous giving, leadership, cheerful mercy. This is a good passage to revisit when you talk about roles and responsibilities within your group, and how group members can serve each other and those outside the group.

*Developing*

10. Review the *Spiritual Gifts Inventory* with the group. Affirm those who have served the group or plugged into a ministry and encourage those who have not that it's never too late. If you have people still struggling with identifying their gifts, encourage them to talk to people who know them well. You might want to share what you've seen in them as well.

*Sharing*

12. Humility is considering others ahead of ourselves. Sympathy is showing genuine care or concern for another's life. Encourage the group to discuss the myriad of ways that these attitudes can be attached to action.

*Surrendering*

14. Have everyone answer the question "HOW are you surrendering your heart?" on the *Personal Health Plan*.

## Session Seven  Living Out This New Life, Part 2

*Connecting*

1. Be sure to have spiritual partners check in with each other at this last meeting. Encourage them to go through the *Personal Health Assessment* together, to assess where they have grown and where they would like to continue to grow. Also encourage them to discuss whether they would like to continue in their mentoring relationship outside of the Bible study.

2. Take a few minutes for group members to share one thing they learned or a commitment they made or renewed during this study. They may also want to share what they enjoyed most about the study and about this group.

   Be prepared to offer some suggestions for resources for answering questions that may arise from this study. Offer other Scripture that relates to the topics studied. Ask your pastor to suggest some helpful books or articles. Advise group members to schedule a meeting with a pastor. Whatever you do, don't let anyone leave with unanswered questions or without the resources to find the answers.

*Growing*

This session covers all of chapters 13 through 16. Consider asking the group to read these passages at home before coming to the group.

3. The example of the persecution of Christians after a terrible fire in Rome gives your group a chance to talk about how submitting to governing authorities (recognizing their authority, paying taxes, obeying the vast majority of laws, etc.) doesn't mean blindly obeying governments when they command something immoral. Protesting unjust laws—and in rare cases refusing to obey them—is consistent with submission. God remains our ultimate authority, even above the government.

4. Paul's examples are rooted in Jewish and Gentile cultural differences about things like eating meat and keeping the Sabbath. Some of the principles he lays out are: 1) Accept those who believe they shouldn't do something you think is okay. Don't quarrel with them or treat them with contempt (14:1, 3). 2) Don't judge those who do things you think aren't okay if those things are genuine gray areas (14:3–4). Other Christians are accountable to God. 3) Take the trouble to form your own convictions (14:5). 4) Be sure that whichever choice you make, you can in good conscience do it "to the Lord" and thank the Lord for it (14:6–8). You are accountable to God too. 5) We will all one day stand before the Lord and give an account for our choices, so make your choices in that light (14:10–12). 6) Don't flaunt your "freedom" in ways that distress a fellow Christian or tempt him to do something he believes is wrong (14:13–16). You shouldn't buckle under

134

someone's judgmental attitude, but if you're causing distress and moral confusion for someone of good will, consider curbing your behavior in their presence. 7) Upright living, peace with one another, and joy are more important than getting your way (14:17).

6. You might want to read aloud each of the principles in the *Leader's Notes* for question 4, talk about how it is rooted in the Bible text, and discuss how it applies to Joe's situation.

## Developing

11. Encourage the group to discuss some practical ways to live as living sacrifices in their day-to-day lives. Living as a living sacrifice requires that we put the Lord first. Some ways include having a daily quiet time, reflecting on Scripture as you commute to work or home, and uttering prayers as you go about daily routines.

12. If time permits, allow one or two people to share how this new discipline of spending daily time in God's Word has transformed their relationship with God.

13. If you haven't already done so, you'll want to take time to discuss the future of your group. You need to talk about whether you will continue together as a group, who will lead, and where you will meet.

As you discuss the future of your group, talk about how well you achieved the goals you made in the *Small Group Agreement*. Address any changes you'd like to make as you move forward.

## Sharing

14. Allow one or two group members to share for a few minutes a testimony about how they helped someone connect in Christian community or shared Jesus with an unbelieving friend or relative.

# DEEPENING
# LIFE TOGETHER
# SERIES

## New Studies Available!

FRUIT OF THE SPIRIT

JAMES

PAUL

PSALMS

RUTH

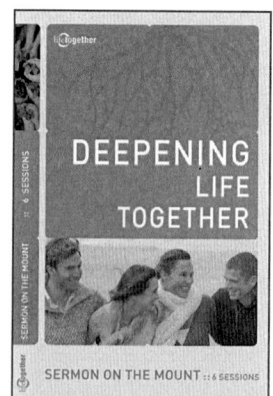

SERMON ON THE MOUNT

*Deepening Life Together* is an innovative approach to group Bible study in a DVD format built on the five biblical purposes: *connecting, growing, developing, sharing, and surrendering.*

Each session includes a traditional study guide and a DVD with insightful teaching from trusted scholars and pastors. Included on each DVD are pre-session training videos for leaders and footage from the bestselling *Jesus Film*.

Lifetogether has developed and sold over 2.5 million copies of bestselling, award-winning curriculum for small groups. This DVD series—perfect for small group ministries, Sunday school classes, and Bible study groups—will improve your worship, fellowship, discipleship, evangelism, and ministry.

# Studies Available:

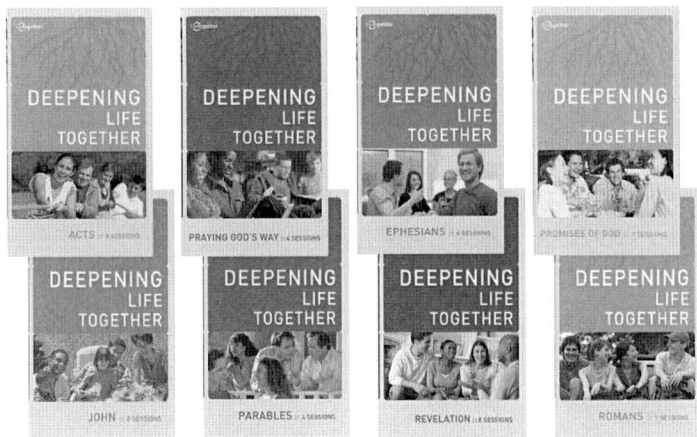

ACTS

PRAYING GOD'S WAY

EPHESIANS

PROMISES OF GOD

JOHN

PARABLES

REVELATION

ROMANS